My Mo

"WATCH OUT FOR THOSE FRENCH GIRLS"

Memoir of a Very Lucky Man

Daniel A. DeCarlo

My Mother Said, "Watch out for Those French Girls"

Edited by Thalya DeMott, Susan Marg, and Brian Gahran

Cover design by Bonnie Beatson, Windward Community College

Interior design and layout by Robert Goodman, Silvercat™, San Diego, CA

Contents

APPENDIX

Dedication

In loving memory of my mom and dad, who in spite of very little education and money, wisely guided our family with common sense and strong faith; and especially to Mother, whose prophetic words to "Watch those French girls" have always put a smile in my heart.

In memory of Genevieve, whose beauty, charm, and wit captured my heart for life. Little did I realize that I would marry the first French girl I met!

To Eric: Having you as my son has profoundly enriched my life from the moment we met, and continues to do so, every day.

To my five siblings: Tony, Evelyn, Victor, Jean, and Neil, who have been my best friends for life; and especially Jean, who has helped me in so many ways.

In memory of Mr. David Rasel, the elementary school principal who rescued me by disbanding the special education class and placing me back in the fourth grade, giving me a second chance at school. I am eternally grateful.

In memory of Mr. John Hulstrunk, shop teacher; and Mr. Jenkins, health education teacher; who were among many who guided me during the formative high school years.

In memory of "Mom" Lominack in Newberry, South Carolina, who provided me with a comforting home when I needed it the most.

In memory of Dr. Jo Piekarz, professor at University of South Carolina, who encouraged me and helped me study and prepare for the Graduate Record Examination.

To a U.S. State Department official whose hint for me to "take a walk" probably saved my life.

In memory of Dr. Joe Mason, Director of DoDDS Europe, for his understanding, support and good advice during some troubled days.

To our American system of government and education which provides opportunities to those who are willing to work and *can* succeed in spite of some difficulties, as the author of this book can attest.

To all the teachers, professors and others who changed the course of my life and made all the difference in who I would become, and to educators everywhere: What would our country be without you?

To Ruth Colby, who was a senior at Kubasaki High School and transcribed essential parts of the original story from my narration on cassette tapes, way back in 1976! Ruth, it has taken me nearly forty years to write and revise this story, but your typing put the project in motion. Thank you, wherever you are.

To caregiver Mary R., whose skill and devoted care brought comfort to my dear Genevieve, and to all the caregivers all over the world who bring comfort to those who are in their last days. You are indeed God's angels on earth.

To Thalya DeMott, whose encouragement and interest in writing this book made it a reality.

To Brian Gahran, my "adopted" son, for his sage advice and wisdom over the years, and his valuable assistance in editing this book and getting it printed.

There are many others who have in one way or another guided, assisted and encouraged me along the way. I wish I could recognize you by name, but I remember you and the positive impact you made on my life. You have my deepest gratitude, and I made it through because of you.

Portrait by Dr. Albert Poirier

Introduction

When individuals set about the task of recording their life events, the recollection process engages the emotions in unforeseeable ways. While involved in the creation of this book, every poignant memory gripped my feelings with the same depth I experienced a lifetime ago. This phenomenon caught me completely by surprise, as it set me on an unexpected journey into reliving my past, as well as relearning from it. There were days where my head hurt and my thoughts were spinning, requiring me to stop everything and regroup until I could start writing again. All matters considered, I found this project both challenging and gratifying.

As the old saying goes, "Truth is stranger than fiction." To my knowledge, everything related in this book is true, although it was necessary to exclude or change a few names. Historical facts intertwine with my narrative, and I encourage further exploration by the curious researcher.

Throughout my adult life, I've collected and scrapbooked a comprehensive archive of photos, articles, and letters which invoke the range from joy to tragedy. News articles clipped a half-century ago are fragile and yellowed with age, filling pages of thick albums. Safeguarding these memories and hoping to share them someday, nearly fifty such volumes have been packed and re-packed to accompany our multiple relocations to many different countries. As my life draws to a close, this weighty stockpile of memorabilia faces a questionable future. My family probably thinks I'd like to take these items with me, but I haven't yet figured out a way. However, knowing that my story has been told will make it a little easier to release my grip.

My dad advised his children, "Try to avoid these three subjects when talking with people: politics, religion, and sex. These are personal and private matters and can be very controversial." As a barber, Dad always knew it would be unwise to share such discussions with his customers, although I'm sure he listened politely to earfuls of other peoples' opinions. "What should I talk about?" I inquired, referring to the first two subjects on his list of three. Of course, I had no idea what sex was or how to talk about it, this not being in a third-grader's scope of understanding. "Talk about ideas, books, food, travel, of better ways to do things, and how you can help people." Although I endeavored to follow Dad's advice, I later got myself embroiled in politics during several traumatic episodes of my life, going to battle against authority as I defended my rights and applied my sense of justice. In the eyes of some people, the international incident I caused in Libya while trying to do the right thing brought embarrassment to my country. Moreover, whether right or wrong, it almost cost me my life. Regardless of consequences, I would do it all again.

ONE

Growing Up Italian-American

My mother, Rose Cardinale, was from Montesano, a hilltop medieval village buttressed by ancient stone walls in southeast Italy. Her parents were employed as farm laborers, owning only their simple home. They had no running water, electricity, indoor toilets, or heating. The town didn't have a plumbing system, and wastewater flowed in gutters alongside the narrow winding cobblestone streets.

In the early 1900s, Rose's parents sought a better life in the United States but were not able to afford passage from Italy for the entire family. Rose's father, Angelo, arrived in the U.S. by steamship in 1909, bringing nineteen-year old Nick, the eldest. In 1920, seventeen-year old Rose arrived with her mother and sister. Immediately upon entry at Ellis Island, Rose's mother required hospitalization for pneumonia, which she caught during the arduous thirty-day crossing. Immigration officers told the ailing Italian woman that deportation was imminent if her health didn't improve. Fortunately my grandma recovered, and she always told us how she would rather have died than endure another miserable ocean crossing! Together they joined their family in Pennsylvania, where Angelo had been working for years as a coal miner in the small town of Washington.

My father, Francesco "Frank" DeCarlo, was about eight years older than my mother Rose. When he was eighteen years old, he, too, emigrated from Italy to the United States. With only a fourth grade education, he went to work in a steel mill.

In those days the shortcut to citizenship was to enlist in the army, and with World War I breaking out in Europe, Frank signed up and was shipped off to active duty in France where he fought in major battles. This included the epic Argonne Forest offensive under General Pershing in 1918, when the war was in its final stages. In only six weeks of fighting the German army in the rough, hilly terrain, the Allies sustained over 26,000 casualties.

Frank was among the wounded in this battle. He was hurt when an explosion threw him into a shell hole. He felt a searing pain in his hand and held it up to see a finger gone. To reduce blood loss he quickly made a tourniquet from his leg wraps and tightened it by twisting the fabric with his bayonet. A few hours later the medics arrived at the battle site to tend the wounded, and they applied a hot iron to cauterize the bleeding. After the armistice he was awarded a Purple Heart.

Frank returned to the U.S. after the war and settled down in the coal mining town of Washington, Pennsylvania. The young veteran, still a bachelor, began his career as a barber. He fit right in, as all the barbers were Italian then. Despite now missing his right ring finger to balance his scissors, he managed very well. He received seven dollars monthly disability for life as compensation for his loss. Dad used to say, "It's not much, but it pays the phone bill." My brothers and I would gather at Dad's feet in rapt attention when he recalled his war stories. He told us about life in the trenches and living with rats and lice. He said the men feared the rats more than the Germans. Almost one hundred years later, his Purple Heart remains in our family as a cherished treasure.

Although I don't recall hearing stories of exactly how my parents met, it may have been at the church where young people socialized. After marrying in 1921, my mother had eight pregnancies in twelve years, from 1922 to 1934. Although two were lost prematurely, we had six healthy children in our family with an average age difference of only a year and a half, so we certainly contributed to the adage regarding prolific-sized Italian families. In order of birth were Tony, Evelyn, Victor, then me, Jean, and Neil. We were all born at home in our parents' bed with the same Italian doctor attending to every one of the deliveries. I fondly

Youngest to oldest: Neil, Jean, Daniel, Victor, Evelyn, Tony.

recall when my brother Neil was born. My younger sister Jean and I were sitting on the steps leading to my parent's bedroom when the doctor came out and said, "Well, kids, you have a baby brother." We almost lost Neil a few years later when he crossed a busy street looking for me and was hit by a car. He recovered, thanks to the resilience of youth.

* * *

Before I was born my parents moved the family from Mill Street, near my aunt's house in the old Italian quarter, to Brown Street to be closer to the center of town and the barber shop where Dad worked. We were the only Italian family in our new neighborhood. Although our previous location was in a rough area, Dad preferred it but deferred to Mom. She believed we children should "grow up in an American neighborhood, because we are in America and my children are Americans."

Our home's three bedrooms were on the second floor. My brothers and I shared a bedroom with two double beds, and the two girls were in a room together. We had a "pee pot" in the hallway for all eight of us to use during the night, because the only bathroom was downstairs on the ground floor. On Saturdays we children helped around the house. We tilled the soil in the back yard to plant vegetables, emptied ash from our coal stove that heated the house, and carried buckets of soapy laundry water from the washtub to the gutter outside. There was always something that needed doing in a six-room, one-bath home.

At twenty-five cents per haircut, Papa earned up to two dollars a day. We couldn't afford a car. To save a nickel on trolley fare, he walked an hour daily to his job at the barber shop. After working for someone else for several years, Papa opened his own non-union shop. Either the union thugs or the mafia—perhaps the same people—kept trying to burn it down, so he converted the basement of our house into his place of business, figuring they wouldn't go so far as to burn down his house. Fortunately, he was right.

I wanted to be like my Dad. When I was four years old, I was playing barber shop under the dining table with my two-year old sister Jean. Getting hold of a scissors I short-cropped her hair and bangs into a random zigzag style. It might have been creative, but it certainly was not a professional job. For my efforts I received a sound spanking from my father, the first one I can remember. I cried. Poor Jean couldn't understand what the fuss was all about, as she liked her new style. It turns out that I was way ahead of my time because the "punk" look became popular fifty years later. After that incident, I didn't pick up another pair of scissors until I was sixteen years old and working as a barber's apprentice.

Mama was a robust woman, taller than Papa, and she cooked, cleaned, ironed, gardened, canned, sewed, and neatly patched our clothes to be handed down and worn again and again. My mother had good taste. She built fireplaces, decorated, dressed well on our meager budget, and was fastidious and dignified. With her Singer treadle sewing machine she mended our clothes and made dresses. She could do and make anything. Mom had no formal education or training, but she had a lot of common sense.

On Sundays our family walked to church together, and afterwards we returned home for the biggest meal of the week. It's amazing how our parents could manage to feed all of us on a barber's earnings. We leisurely ate from noon until four o'clock. Our bounty included our own garden-fresh tomatoes, cabbage, corn, carrots, peppers, parsley, squash, cherries, figs, and more. In our back yard we raised chickens, rabbits, and pigeons. There was no point becoming attached to these animals and giving them names, as they would eventually become dinner. We never had pet dogs or cats because we couldn't afford to feed them.

At the start of every year Papa bought a young turkey to feed and fatten for Thanksgiving, and by November we had a bird large enough to feed the entire family and then some. By day we kept the turkey securely tethered by the ankle to a concrete drain lid so it couldn't fly away, but it had plenty of slack to graze and scratch in the yard. At night we moved the turkey inside, and it bedded down in a cozy straw pile in the basement.

Before Thanksgiving one year, Papa skillfully sharpened his butcher knife, as a barber would know how to do, with a loud rhythmic scraping back and forth on the stone. We'll never know how that turkey could have understood what the sound meant, for when Papa opened the basement door, an unearthly scream and twenty pounds of charging feathered fury greeted him. That turkey knocked him flat out of breath as it burst into the yard and attempted its escape over the fence, dragging along the concrete drain cover. With Papa in hot pursuit, the frantic bird was apprehended but continued fighting like there was no tomorrow, thrashing wildly as Papa strung its feet to the clothesline. With one skilled move, the bird's head clunked into a bucket. At the same moment, the bindings holding its feet loosened just enough for freedom to beckon one last time, and the whole headless bundle of flapping feathers spun wildly in circles, blood shooting everywhere — on my dad, the fence, the neighbor's house, and across the side of our house, covering the windows and doors. Mama was furious, but she prepared a wonderful meal as usual. We ate late because we had to clean up, but it was a Thanksgiving we never forgot.

Another bird also made a lasting impression on us. One early spring day, Dad was walking to work when he heard a chirp. He stopped, listened, and heard it again—chirp, chirp! Looking down into a pile of snow, he saw a shivering purple creature with its beak gaping open. He picked up the tiny chick, put it in his overcoat pocket, and continued on his way. The ball of pinfeathers and fluff revived after Dad placed it in a sunny window and fed it crumbs from his homemade Italian sandwich. That night Dad came home and announced, "Here, kids, I have something for you," handing over a paper bag dotted with air holes. When we opened the package the one-eyed purple chick greeted us with his chirpy "Twee-Twee," and that's what we named him. He grew up to be a big fighting rooster, but he was truly our pet, the only pet we ever had. He followed us around and answered to his name. We looked forward to playing with him after school every day.

After church one Sunday, our family sat down to our customary meal for that special day of the week. We feasted on delicious homemade meatballs and pasta, a variety of vegetables, fruit, nuts, and what we thought was a roasted chicken. As always, we finished our meal with crispy celery sticks dipped in olive oil, salt and pepper, before declaring we were going out to play with Twee-Twee. At this, Mother shook her head sadly and spoke to us in Italian, explaining, "My poor, dear little children, you just got through eating Twee-Twee." I can hear her words to this day. Neil, Jean and I cried for hours and hours.

Mondays were known as "spinach night" in the DeCarlo house. I absolutely could not stomach the idea of eating a mushy pile of boiled leaves. As Mother insisted that we eat our spinach or nothing at all, I often went to bed hungry on Mondays. I must admit that I occasionally slipped into the garden at night when the tomatoes were in season and had my fill. Vic, on the other hand, ate his spinach, and perhaps this is why he grew taller than me.

Every week Mother baked fragrant loaves of bread, and on Saturdays she made delicious pies from scratch. When I was growing up there was no such thing as an instant baking mix, and ingredients were fresh grown and wholesome. One particular Saturday, Victor and I got into a squabble over whether it was his turn to listen to his favorite radio show, Mr. District Attorney, or my turn to listen to my favorite, Gang Busters. Both shows were broadcast in the same time slot on different stations, and we only had one radio.

As our skirmish turned into a battle, Vic chased me through the kitchen and out the back door. When we crashed onto the porch where Mother had carefully placed the pies on the top railing to cool, the pies flew! Lemon meringue, chocolate cream, and bright red cherry pies lay upside down on the ground ruined. In this era we didn't have much violence in the movies, but there was plenty of action to be found in our own back yard.

The fight fizzled as we foresaw our parents' wrath for such wasteful and unnecessary destruction. Running to hide in the tomato patch, we prepared our survival strategy: when Papa came home and whistled for us, Vic would enter the house through the back door while I went in the front. This way, he wouldn't be able to whoop us both at the same time, and one of us, or so we thought, would be spared.

Soon enough we heard Papa's first shrill whistle, followed by another. By the third one we knew it was our last chance to show our sorry faces. When Vic went in the back door, as planned, Papa nabbed him. I heard Vic crying out, although I was already upstairs, hiding under the bed. Papa wasted no time finding me and dragged me out by the ankles. Then it was my turn to cry.

After the pie incident, Vic and I became buddies. We no longer fought, and he even helped me with my homework. None of us kids had any emotional scars from our parents' disciplining, which they used only when necessary to keep order in their home.

Our parents were very loving, and we always knew how deeply they cared for us.

Another ritual occurred each fall when Dad's order of forty boxes of wine grapes arrived. Our basement distillery included a homemade wine press and two large wooden barrels to ferment and store the wine. I suspected this set-up was illegal because it was covered with large blankets. We never talked about it, although everyone knew Italians made their own wine. Crushing the grapes with our feet was a family event. We took off our shoes and socks, rolled up our pant legs, and took turns smashing the grapes, giggling uncontrollably at the delightful squishy feeling between our toes! Tony, Victor and Dad loaded up the press with the partially smashed grapes and then pressed them until every drop was squeezed out of the pulp. The juice was poured into pans and then transferred to the barrels where it aged for six weeks. We mixed the leftover grape skins and stems into the garden to provide nutrients for the soil. It was fun teamwork, and Dad had wine to drink and to share when Italian friends visited throughout the year.

No one ever told us we were poor, as everyone else in the neighborhood lived as we did and worked hard. Somehow or other we made ends meet. In addition to our chores we boys all worked from an early age, and the money we earned went to mother for safekeeping or household needs.

At eight years old I had my first job as a shoeshine boy in my cousin Angelo's shop. All the shoemakers were Italian. My brothers, too, worked for Angelo at ten cents a shine. We also had newspaper routes and collected scrap iron, empty bottles, and newspapers to sell at the junk dealer. We picked corn, tomatoes, pumpkins, peppers and beans for an Italian man who had several cultivated acres located directly behind his produce market on Chestnut Avenue. We affectionately called him Dago John. However, if anyone called us "Dago" it was reason to fight. Tony had to rescue us from scuffles a number of times. Thank God for big brothers.

On Saturdays I loved going to the movies to see Tom Mix or Hopalong Cassidy, the cowboy heroes of many early Westerns. One time upon arriving at the theater I handed my ten cents to the box office lady who looked scornfully down at my hard-earned coins and said, "Sorry, it's eleven cents now." I pleaded that I didn't know the price had gone up. Sternly, she retorted, "It was in the paper." "We don't get the paper," I stammered. "Too bad," she snapped back.

Walking nearly three miles home to get a penny from my mother and returning to the theater, it never occurred to me to ask someone on the street for change. Begging from strangers was unheard of in my experience. But to this day I will pick up a penny from the ground no matter what.

Sometimes I spent my hard-earned money on presents. One January day I was walking by the dollar store when I spotted in the window the most beautiful sparkling set of China dishes I had ever seen. In an instant I knew they would be perfect for Mother's Day. Sure, they were expensive, and I didn't have twenty-three dollars on hand to pay for them, but I had a plan. I approached my cousin Dolores, who worked in the store, and asked if I'd be able to purchase the dishes by making payments over time. Neither Dolores nor I had every heard of layaway, but she agreed.

For the next five months I dutifully brought my hard earned nickels and dimes to the store, and Dolores and I kept an exact tally of the funds paid and the balance due. The day before Mother's Day, I was short by $1.30 and completely despondent as I worked in Angelo's shoe repair shop, hoping to miraculously raise the money I needed. Then the butcher from next door brought me ten pairs of shoes to clean for ten cents each. These were not regular shoes, but butcher's boots covered with dried blood, grease, and feathers. I rubbed and scrubbed and polished until my arms ached. For my hard work the butcher gave me a dollar plus a quarter tip. I was still a nickel short when in came two "colored girls," as we referred to African-Americans then, who wanted their shoes shined. As I worked, the two girls giggled, "Look at his long eyelashes!" I was so embarrassed because no one had ever said this to me, but henceforth my eyelashes were an asset to be employed as a flirting tool. And I finally had enough money for the box of thirty-six gold-rimmed China dishes! Rushing to the dollar store, I arrived just before closing time.

On the big day, when Mother opened her surprise gift with anticipation, Jean, only a toddler then, suddenly reached in to pick up a teacup and immediately dropped it. To my horror, the first thing out of the box lay in pieces at my feet. My heart almost stopped as I thought of what I had gone through to get those dishes, but Mother was able to calm the situation. I got over it, but I never forgot the sound of the cup crashing on the floor. Eighty years later, Jean remembers dropping the cup. The dishes, greatly cherished, had plenty of good use over the years. After Mom passed away I received the three remaining pieces from the set, which I use to this day.

***

My school days started well. On my first day of first grade, all the kids were scared and crying except me. I felt proud when the teacher, Miss Burns, pointed to me and said, "Look at Danny—he's not crying."

Things soon went sour. A few weeks into the year I found an empty glass jar sticking out of the dirt in an alleyway on my way home. I cleaned it up and discovered it was an inkwell. The next day I showed it to some classmates and informed them I was going to give it to our teacher. I really wanted to impress her. Before I could present it to her, the boys reported that I had an inkwell and she demanded to see it. I explained how I found it but she didn't believe me and angrily accused me of stealing it from the school, although we didn't use inkwells in first grade. She stood towering over me, one hand planted on her hip and the other sternly pointing to the corner of the room where I shuffled over to hide my face in pitiful shame. I knew I had been punished unjustly, and from then on, I hated school. I don't recall another thing from first grade—except the other kids poking fun at me for having to stand in the corner.

I don't remember anything from second or third grade, either. Fourth grade was a different matter. Whether it was because I was a terrible student or a terror in the classroom, my outlook on education crumbled.

I was notorious for my deadly aim with spit-wads. I'd roll paper into solid little clumps to wet in my mouth and then launch them via rubber bands. Proudly, I must say, I rarely missed my target. But a very regrettable prank on my fourth grade teacher, Miss Longway, set me back a long way. As the other kids in my class egged me on, I soaked a string in black ink and tied it between the rows of desks by the doorway. When Miss Longway entered the room, the inky string snapped across her ankles, staining her stockings and skin. When my classmates ratted me out, she furiously sent me to Mr. Moore, the principal, to receive a sound paddling with a board made precisely for that purpose. I told myself I would be strong and not cry, but he kept paddling until I couldn't hold onto my resolve. The moment I cried out in pain, Mr. Moore stopped. The next time I went into Mr. Moore's office for a paddling, I cried out loudly at the first whack.

I failed the fourth grade and had to repeat it the following year with the same teacher...Miss Longway. I knew I was doomed. Midway through the year, the eagle-eyed teacher caught me cheating during a spelling test by hiding a book on my lap. She dragged me to the principal's office for another red-hot paddling. Seventy-five years later, I found it comforting to learn of a study that showed that spelling ability has no bearing on intelligence. Apparently, no one knew this at the time.

The spelling-test incident put the nail in the coffin of my second attempt at fourth grade, as Miss Longway had me declared irreversibly incorrigible and placed in "Mrs. Bash's Dumbbell Room" with other juvenile delinquents. The Dumbbell Room, similar to what was later called "Special Ed," represents a very low point in my childhood. I sensed it meant that I wasn't expected to go very far in life. Instead of learning reading, writing, and arithmetic, we wiled away the hours doing arts and crafts. However, I found comfort in working with my hands. I still have a few of the items I made, including a pair of miniature hand-stitched leather boxing gloves. These are displayed in a framed glass case hanging on the wall over my desk and serve as a lifetime reminder of where I was and how I somehow made the best of it.

My dumbbell class incarceration lasted at least a year, and then something wonderful happened. A new principal, Mr. Rasel, began his term at the school and immediately disbanded the dumbbell class. Now I was back in the fourth grade for the third time...fortunately not with Miss Longway, but a new teacher, Miss McClure. I was now two years older and much bigger than my classmates! Yet this time I excelled because I wanted to impress a cute blonde girl in class. On Valentine's Day our class exchanged handmade valentines with each other. Inspired by love, I gave the blonde girl the one I made especially for her, and eagerly awaited her response...which never came. Everyone in the class received a valentine, but there were none for me, not even one. I left heartbroken, crying all the way home that no one loved me.

Later that night, there was an unexpected knock at our door. The friend who walked home from school with me had told his parents of my anguish, and he and his parents had trudged up and down hills in ankle-deep snow to deliver a valentine for me! I kept that valentine for years. Unfortunately, it was lost when I moved away after college, but I have never forgotten the kindness of my classmate.

Although fourth grade was a bad experience, I was able to skip the fifth and seventh grades by going to summer school. By the eighth grade I had caught up with the other kids my age.

***

One Sunday when I was about ten years old, our cousins had come over for lunch and the adults retired to the living room for

My brothers and sisters in 1984: Tony, Evelyn, Victor, Jean, Neil, and me (photo added later)

leisurely conversation. This room was off limits to the children, but we didn't mind because we went to listen to the big upright radio in the hallway. About two o'clock a frantic announcer cut into the program with an emergency news statement, saying that the Japanese had attacked Pearl Harbor. We didn't understand what this meant so I ran to ask my Dad, interrupting his conversation with our cousin Angelo. Initially, he scolded me, but I finally got his attention.

The news of the Japanese attack of December 7, 1941 was shocking and unbelievable. As Dad listened to the broadcast, he confidently slapped his thigh and declared, "We'll lick 'em in two weeks!" I can still hear his words to this day. But the war lasted four years and millions of lives were lost. The Pearl Harbor attack is known in history as "The Day That Will Live in Infamy," and it changed our lives and everyone else's around the world.

I distinctly remember air raid drills with lights out and shades drawn. Convoys of trucks carrying soldiers, and tanks with armaments passed through our little town. Everyone contributed their extra scrap iron and aluminum for the war effort. I made many trips to the collection yard pulling my little red wagon loaded with scrap metal to be melted down and turned into airplane wings and who knows what. Tony soon went off to war, and I know our parents must have given silent prayers for his safety.

After war was declared against Germany and Japan, my fourth grade teacher instructed us to henceforth keep our right hands over our hearts while saying the Pledge of Allegiance, rather than the previous custom of saluting the flag by raising and extending our straightened right arm and hand. We were too young to understand our teacher's explanation of the Nazi salute. But we certainly grasped the fact that we were at war.

TWO

Mother's Prediction

In 1943 my parents uprooted us from our rural Pennsylvania town of 26,000 to Newark, New Jersey, an urban center of 400,000. What an adjustment for a thirteen-year old! I quickly realized we had left far behind the idyllic country life of fishing, hunting, picking wild berries, and milking cows at my uncle's farm. Our new neighborhood was a hubbub of noisy vendors hawking their wares and unruly mobsters pursuing their gambling and racketeering interests. But Mama said there was little opportunity for her children in Pennsylvania... only steel mills and coal mines. Neither of my folks were afraid of change, believing we shouldn't get stuck in one place if we could do better elsewhere.

Dad got a janitorial job at Tung Sol Lamp and Bulb Factory. He often stayed after hours to watch the machinists and ask questions, so he could learn to do what they did. He became a machine operator and remained happily with Tung Sol until retirement.

Initially, we rented a fifth floor walk-up in Little Italy. My Uncle Nick had a grocery store nearby, and we were in close proximity to my aunt's preferred church. Papa Angelo, my maternal grandpa, lived with them after Grandma passed away in her eighties. Papa Angelo had worked in the coal mines in Pennsylvania while raising his family, but later worked for the railroad. He was always sharply dressed with a shiny gold pocket watch in his vest. Every two weeks he walked the six blocks to our house for my dad to give him a haircut. To cross busy Orange Avenue, he waved his walking cane in the air to stop the traffic. He spoke only Italian and lived to be at least 102 years old. All four of us brothers have the middle name "Angelo" in his honor.

My dad wanted his boys to be barbers. So, with the exception of Victor, the smart one who became an engineer, we learned to cut hair. For me, this paid off when I was in college, as I earned extra change on weekends in my dorm room. Although Tony worked as a barber for a short time, he pursued his true calling, becoming a very good machinist. Neil was an appliance repairman before he became a record-breaking salesman in that field. None of us followed Dad into his trade, but he was proud of our success in our chosen vocations, nevertheless.

A few months after moving to Newark, my parents bought a home in a slightly better area. When I finished at McKinley Junior High, it was decided that I should go to a boy's technical school because I "wasn't good with books." Nowadays, I would have been diagnosed as dyslexic.

In my first year at the tech school, my ninth grade wood shop teacher almost got killed by a student. Mr. Hulstrunk was a good but strict teacher, and I enjoyed building and making things in his class. One day Mr. Hulstrunk asked a disruptive student to be quiet and pay attention. Instead of settling down, the boy jeered, "Make me!" He then jumped up with a pistol in his hand and started shooting. Mr. Hulstrunk ran out the door in a panic with the student chasing him, gun in hand. The rest of us instinctively fell to the floor.

Miraculously, no one was hurt. In no time at all, police were everywhere. The boy evasively told police he'd tossed the gun in the gutter. Well, everything that went into the gutter ended up in the sewer trap, and that's where they easily found the incriminating evidence.

The prosecutor interviewed the entire class as witnesses. He delved into the details of what had occurred and requested we testify. In time, the court found our classmate guilty and sentenced him to three years at a work farm. To my utter amazement and his credit, Mr. Hulstrunk pleaded with the judge on behalf of the perpetrator. He believed the boy would become a hardened criminal at the work farm and recommended that the judge sentence him to three years of home duty instead. Further, Mr. Hulstrunk said he would feed, clothe and support the young man under his own roof. I couldn't believe the charity of this man who would take into his own home a juvenile delinquent who had tried to kill him. The judge, too, appeared surprised and touched by this sincere gesture. He explained, however, that the law did not permit him to do such, and the sentence was passed.

Mr. Jenkins, the health teacher, also befriended me. Mr. Jenkins had been the 1936 Olympic wrestling champion for his weight class, and I tagged along regularly with him to the New York Athletic Club where he worked out. He not only taught me some good wrestling moves, but he also introduced me to Charles Atlas, Joe Louis, Arthur Donovan and "Two Ton" Tony Galento, who knocked out Joe Louis in their first fight. In their rematch six months later, Joe Louis knocked him out only a minute into the first round. I'm sure the betting was heavy on that fight, and some lost a fortune! At the local YMCA I also met Tony Zale, the world champ middleweight. It wasn't until years later that I realized how fortunate I was to meet these history-making athletes.

The YMCA in those days was an interesting place to hang out and work out. Given that the pool facilities were men only, no one wore swimwear. Everyone was very nonchalant about being nude, and not just in the locker room, where you'd expect it, but also at the indoor pool. No one felt shy or made jokes. It was just accepted as normal. I'm sure this custom would now be considered quite peculiar.

My extracurricular school activities kept me busy, too. I was active in the student council and determined to be student body president. Surprisingly, I won the election the year I ran. Perhaps it was the hand-rolled cigarettes with "Vote for DeCarlo" stamped on the paper. I never smoked any, but the boys who did said they tasted awful. Luckily no one was poisoned, as I had used the wrong kind of ink.

I advocated for the first dance ever held at the school, and the student council and administration approved the plans. As the dance was underway, I got word that some guys from another school were going to rob us of the entry fees collected at the door. I rushed to warn Mr. Jenkins, who carried the money bag securely under his arm at the dance, and he called the police. When they showed up a group of boys left the dance. This was a close call! The would-be robbers didn't trouble us again.

I enjoyed sports, as well as planning and organizing special events. It was surprising to me that our school didn't have any sports teams, so I decided to do something about it. Working again with Mr. Jenkins and the student council, we started up intramural teams for boxing, wrestling, and basketball. The students were inner city tough guys who'd been around, and they swore an awful lot. I didn't pick up the habit because it didn't fit with the way I was brought up.

I also had a job at a garment factory. At one point I was thinking about quitting school to work full time to earn enough money to buy a car. Fortunately for me, Mr. Hulstrunk was watching out for me. He encouraged me to stay in school and arranged my transfer to Barringer High, the third oldest public high school in the entire country. Although I was behind in credits for reading, writing, and math, with the encouragement of kind teachers I began to catch up. The gorgeous English teacher, Miss Fowler, had the adoration of all the boys. She and others gave me extra writing assignments for practice.

Even while I attended Barringer High, I remained close to Mr. Hulstrunk. On Saturdays I worked with him in his side business, fabricating and repairing doors and windows. On Saturday nights, I was often found at the Hulstrunk home, which he and his family transformed into a musical extravaganza. His three children played different instruments and his wife excelled on piano. Their daughter made all-state trumpet player in New Jersey. I learned to play the saxophone and had a great time. Mr. Hulstrunk was a good man, a guiding light in my life with a truly generous heart.

After school on weekdays I also worked at a shop rehabbing surplus machinery and equipment discarded by the government and military. I was about fifteen or sixteen years old, and Mr. Rowe, the owner, trusted me to run the register when he was out of the store. He praised me, saying, "I can rely on Daniel, I'm lucky to have him." Mr. Rowe also taught me how to drive. Eventually, I had my own car, a first in my family.

Although I was good in the trades, I needed to catch up on books. I applied myself to this goal at Barringer High, and I made National Honor Society my senior year. I also joined the wrestling team, the Thespians, chess club, science club, and played sax and clarinet in band. In 1949 I graduated when I was nineteen years old.

***

Finished with high school and having some money in my pocket, I bought my first car, a 1932 Dodge, for ninety dollars. I painted it, fixed the transmission and clutch, used it for six months, and then sold it to my brother Victor for a hundred dollars. Vic then drove it off to college in New York.

My Sunday school class on a picnic in 1950

I replaced the '32 Dodge with another Dodge, a '36 sedan. I taught Sunday school to seven-year olds and could fit them all into my car when we went for picnics! There weren't any seat belts or any laws on how many people you could cram into a car. I shudder when I think about it now.

Cars, however, couldn't be my whole life. At Mr. Hulstrunk's urging, I enrolled at Bob Jones University in South Carolina. I was interested in a young lady who was in her senior year there, and we wanted to be on the same campus. When she graduated and moved on, I transferred to Newberry College, a small Lutheran school in Newberry, South Carolina, where I earned my degree in secondary education.

The town of Newberry was a cotton mill town. The gentry lived in the center with their own city-supported youth center featuring movies and dances. They were the privileged folks. The mill workers and their children living in small communities around the perimeter were entirely excluded and had no activities or sports available to them. As if called to a cause, I rented a Masonic hall with my own money for thirty-five dollars a month and organized a car service to transport these kids to their own newly formed Young People's Fellowship Club. We enjoyed film cartoons, games, slide shows, baked goods, board games, music and sing-a-longs, art and voice lessons, and watermelon parties! A theater owner donated bags of popcorn when we showed films. I had a wonderful time with these kids, and they looked forward to weekend nights at the clubhouse.

I continued to involve myself with the community. Farther into the outskirts of Newberry were shantytowns housing cotton pickers and farmhands. These were the poorest of the poor who worked the hardest of all, bending their backs in the hot sun, laden with heavy bags of cotton. Their children would sit on rustic porches or play in the dirt roads. It was heartbreaking for me to see these impoverished black youths with no organized sports or recreational programs for them to enjoy. I befriended a few of the ministers. They agreed to make announcements in church regarding activities for the children, who soon joined me in forming softball teams, throwing horseshoes, playing tug-of-war, and having sack races. I purchased bats, balls, and gloves, and we played ball in an open field of crabgrass and mostly dirt. For a treat, we churned fresh cold ice cream from an old-fashioned ice cream maker I had borrowed. The kids called me "Mr. Dan," and we greatly enjoyed our Saturdays together.

Integration, however, had not yet come to Newberry, and the different races kept to themselves. One day at the square in the center of town, I met up with one of the ministers coming out of the bank. We greeted each other warmly with a handshake and conversed for a few minutes. As we said good-bye and turned to walk in different directions, a police car pulled up, and two big cops stepped purpose-fully out of the car. Walking towards me, they adjusted their gun belts menacingly and demanded, "What are you doing shakin' a nigger's hand?" I was stunned speechless for a moment before telling them that "Mr. Smith" was my friend. "Where you from? What're you doin' here?" I said I was a college student at Newberry. They spoke gruffly. "You better remember this: we don't shake niggers' hands down here, and we don't call them 'mister.'"

Some of the shantytown kids

I can still see these men in my memory, and I feel the shock of their words to this day. This was at the time that three northern men disappeared in Mississippi. Months later their bodies were found buried in an earthen dam.

During my undergraduate days I paid most of my tuition on a working scholarship. I was a busboy in the dining hall, and late at night I cleaned restrooms in the dorm. The older graduate students said their bathrooms had never been so clean. I had to make ends meet in order to get through college. Among my other jobs I went door-to-door selling Electrolux vacuums, bibles, and magazine subscriptions.

After a time I moved out of the dorm to save money, and lived in a back office of the Masonic Hall I rented as a clubhouse for the kids' activities. The building didn't have a heating system, and the winters were especially cold. Night after night I shivered on a small cot, wrapped in piles of blankets. In the freezing mornings I washed and shaved in icy tap water. By chance a trip to the college infirmary with a bad case of flu improved my situation. The nurse there, upon learning of my living conditions, suggested I contact her recently widowed sister-in-law, now living alone. Following up I went to meet Mrs. Lominack, a delightful elderly lady, and we came to an arrangement. She provided me with my own bedroom and bath in her comfortable home, and I helped her around the house and garden. She also appreciated the security of having someone else in the house at night. We got along very well, and she became so much like a second mother to me, I called her "Mom."

One night while we were having fish dinner she began coughing uncontrollably. Although she insisted that everything would be okay if she could just lie down for a rest, I was very concerned and phoned her son across town. He immediately came and took her to the hospital, where doctors extracted a small bone that had gotten stuck in her throat. The hospital kept her several days, and I knew what a serious accident this could have been, if she were alone. I'm just glad I was there to help.

Mrs. Lominack lived another eighteen years and helped other college students who needed a place to stay. We remained in contact after I graduated and moved away.

It seems that I had to expend twice the effort compared to others to get through college. I studied hard and had kind professors.

In particular, a Dr. Piekarz helped me greatly. I wouldn't have made it without her interest and support. A conscientious educator can make a life-altering difference in their students' lives, and my teachers were an enormous influence on me.

On graduation day, as I accepted my degree and walked off the stage, to my great surprise I spotted Mr. and Mrs. Hulstrunk in the audience! They had driven 1,500 miles to attend the ceremony. This great teacher, who took an interest in a "slow" student in high school and encouraged me to study hard, transfer to a regular high school, and go to college, was now here to share one of the most exciting events in my life. I so admired him. With all he had done for me, he inspired me to become a teacher and dedicate myself to helping and encouraging young people. He was the right person at that time and place in my life, and I was deeply honored by his and his wife's presence. I greatly cherished this couple, who became life-long friends.

I still wasn't done with my schooling. After graduating from Newberry College I joined the master's program at the University of South Carolina, pursuing my degree in public school administration. My inspiration to acquire a second degree, in Library Science, was stirred by the process of spending long hours absorbed in reading and research in the university libraries, when I learned to love good books. I just wish I had started sooner.

To pay for my tuition and cover living expenses, I worked during Christmas and summer breaks. I had a railroad job, loading boxcars with mail on the graveyard shift for $1.35 an hour, which was good pay. I was promoted to the roundhouse, a position that made me feel very powerful: I'd throw a switch and turn a 500-ton locomotive around on the tracks, caboose and all. My least favorite part of the job was the unnerving responsibility of rousting replacement engineers from sleep when someone couldn't make it for their day's route. I'd pound on their doors in the middle of the night. If they didn't answer, I was authorized to enter with a key, shake them awake, and require them to sign a roster acknowledging that I'd been there. Fortunately, none of the engineers took a punch at me for startling them. Still, walking the dark streets of Hoboken in the wee hours made me very uneasy. Although I felt a hard worker could build a secure future with the railroad, I was determined to earn my college degree.

While doing my graduate work at the University of South Carolina, I worked as Dean of Men and Recreational Director at the Will Lou Grey Opportunity School. This was a second-chance school for Korean War veterans, dropouts, and marginal students of widely varying ages. Some were handicapped, and most were poorly educated. Almost 99 percent of the veterans had not received their high school diploma. The G.I. Bill subsidized their education at Will Lou Grey, enabling them to graduate. I identified with these men and their difficulties, knowing my own life would have been completely different if I hadn't been given so many second chances, for which I felt a great debt of gratitude. One of my responsibilities was to keep sixty rather undisciplined men on track with their daily lives. I slept in the dorm, and on several occasions, had to break up late-night fights between residents who didn't get along.

Applying myself fully to the challenge of my work, the staff and I rebuilt the dilapidated bowling alley, rented buses for educational field trips including a visit to the gorgeous Cypress Gardens, held a Valentine's dance, took them fishing, and put on a variety show to highlight the talents of many students who could sing, dance, and play instruments. On Sundays we assembled interdenominational church services during which the students quietly read the theological literature of their choice. We also organized graduation ceremonies and the after-parties. It was great fun, but South Carolina was segregated until the 1960s, and this "Opportunity School" was all white. I would have done it differently, but this was the way of life in the South. There were no other options.

***

After finishing my education I wanted to see the world, so I began applying for overseas teaching positions. In the springtime of 1958, six credits away from my Library Science degree, I was summoned from my dorm for a long distance call that would shape my future and bring unimaginable adventures. The operator had a telegram for me. "Congratulations!" she read. "You have been selected to teach in France for the coming school year." This was the news I had been waiting for! Breathless with excitement, I accepted.

I had long dreamed of going to Europe, driven by my father's stories of a different way of life, of rich history steeped in culture. I yearned to know its spectacular cities, famous museums, medieval towns, and gastronomic delights! In my dad's opinion the old country was just old, but to me it held great promises yet to unfold.

I immediately called my folks at home in New Jersey. I hadn't seen Mother in over six months, but when she answered, I blurted out the news of my teaching assignment in France. There was a long silence, then a sigh. In Italian, her only words were, "Oh, son, you'd better watch out for those French girls." I was so surprised. It was the furthest thing from my mind. Little did we realize the meaning of those words, and how her prediction would come true!

I was now officially hired by the Department of Defense Dependent Schools, or DoDDS, also known as Department of Defense Overseas Schools System. After processing my overseas-transfer paperwork at Ft. Jackson and packing for departure from New York, I had to make one stop... in good old Washington, Pennsylvania. I wanted to look up the elementary school principal who disbanded Miss Bash's dumbbell room, thus giving me a second chance in life. Who knows where I'd have ended up if he hadn't done that! I hitchhiked from South Carolina in no time. Although I had forgotten his name, the secretary at the superintendent's office checked the files and located a Mr. Rasel, just the man I was looking for. I immediately took a taxi to the school where he was then working and found him in a classroom arranging supplies for the coming school year. I introduced myself and asked if we could go to his office to sit and talk.

Seated comfortably, I showed him a copy of my master's thesis and read the dedication out loud: "To an unknown elementary principal who saw fit to dissolve an occupational class for the 'mentally retarded' and who placed this class back into the school, thus giving the author of this study a new start in life." I asked if he recalled doing this, and he did remember it vaguely. Thanking him profusely, I told him I made this trip especially to see him in person and express my sincere gratitude. His decision some twenty years ago made such a positive impact that it changed my future. He choked up and gave me a big hug to thank me in return for my time and effort. We visited for a while to chat about the educational system, and parted with warm wishes.

I then had to travel via my thumb to New Jersey. About halfway home, a man driving a big new Chrysler picked me up. When I commented that all the driving controls were located on the steering wheel, he explained that the car was custom ordered, as he was paralyzed from the waist down from an accident. He said he couldn't walk but his driving was good. As we were cruising smoothly along the turnpike the new car suddenly began to make alarming noises and the steering was difficult to control. He exclaimed, "I've blown a tire!" Pulling off to the side, I changed the tire in no time flat. As we continued on our way, he commented how lucky he was to have picked me up. He felt that he would have been stranded on the highway all night and half the day, as no one would have stopped for him, nor could he have walked to a call box to get help. One never knows the good things you can do in life.

My family was at the airport to see me off. After all the hugs and goodbyes, Mother sent me on my way with these wise parting words: "Cuando tu beve, manja." When you drink, eat. Again, Mother's homespun wisdom left its mark, and I soon put these words into practice. From that time on, when I had an alcoholic beverage in my hand I made sure I could reach food with the other.

And so an excited twenty-eight year old anxious to arrive in "the old country" started a new beginning.

THREE

Paris, Love, and Kidnapping

As soon as my plane touched down in France, the beauty of the countryside captivated me. I went through a whole roll of film just traveling from the airport to downtown Paris! My first morning I reported to Rue Marbeuf, in the American office building housing the staff of the Judge Advocate General, or JAG, the Civilian Personnel Office, or CPO, and the PX, or exchange. In a room of about fifty newly recruited teachers from the States, the sergeant in charge rattled off names and assignments. When everyone had been called except three men and me, the sergeant said. "Now, let's see. You four are going to . . . " He paused, and we stopped breathing, before he continued, "You men are staying in Paris and will be located at the American Paris High School." We all gave a joyful yell in unison.

I wanted to get my film developed right away but had arranged lunch with a new acquaintance, Robert. As I waited for him at the main entrance of the building, I looked around impatiently. Nearby a young woman with bright eyes and short dark hair glanced at her watch from time to time. I wasn't the smooth type with the ladies, nor practiced in any irresistible opening lines, but I approached her, asking if she knew whether the PX had a film processing service. She answered in perfect English with a beautiful French accent. This led to discussion of the weather, Paris, and our disappointment that neither of our friends seemed to be showing up. Getting hungry, I suggested, "Look, if our friends don't show up, how about the two of us having lunch together?" I wasn't usually quick on the draw, but I sure was fast this time. As we headed for a restaurant across the street, she politely said,

"I hope you don't mind being a bit rushed, as I have to get back to work."

At lunch I learned that this most attractive woman went by the name Genevieve, and she worked at JAG as a translator. I asked if I might call her sometime, and she kindly agreed. Although I was quite anxious waiting for an appropriate time to call, the following week wasn't too soon, I thought. But when I called, to my disappointment, her co-workers told me she was not in, that she was ill. This, I thought, was a classic brush-off, the universal stalling tactic.

I'm not easily discouraged, however, and I called again and again. Week after week, I was given the same answer: "Genevieve is ill, and she is not at work." Finally, I reached her two months later when she had returned to work. I learned she had really been ill and gone to her mother's to recuperate. French civil servants have a very liberal sick leave policy. "Will you have dinner with me?" I tentatively inquired. "I'd be delighted," she responded. "How about this Friday?" I asked. "Why, yes, indeed," she replied. With a sigh of relief, I heard Mother's words about watching out for those French girls.

I put my heart and soul into planning our first dinner date. Since I was a novice about wine, liquor, and multi-course meals, to say the least, and traditional South Carolina fare cannot be compared with world-famous French cuisine. I bought a copy of Fodor's Guide to France and read everything I could about aperitifs, red and white wines, and after-dinner drinks, such as cognac. Knowing that the French drink with dinner, and not having had a drop of alcohol in years—South Carolina being a dry state—I was concerned I'd be under the table before the meal was half over. But I was determined to impress my special date with my knowledge. I wasn't going to be a country bumpkin in Paris, of all places. I felt nervously excited, but it helped to know I had done my homework.

At five o'clock I met Genevieve at her office building and suggested we stop at one of the cafes on the Champs-Elysées for an aperitif. In my best attempt at being suave and sophisticated, I boldly asked, "What would you like? A Martini Rosso, a Vermouth? You name it and I'll order it for you." To my astonishment, she preferred something light—sans alcohol. This couldn't be true! I perceived all French people as wine connoisseurs. I tried again. "Something a little stronger?" "No thank you," she replied while sipping her orange drink. So, did I pick up the clue? No! I chose a red Vermouth. As I felt the Vermouth warming my esophagus, I remembered Mother's warning: "When you drink, eat." But the cafe didn't serve hors d'oeuvres. I hoped a snack would somehow appear, when a boy walked by peddling peanuts on the street. Thanks to a well-timed bag of peanuts—well, two bags—I didn't embarrass myself.

Having an aperitif is a very enjoyable and relaxing French tradition. One takes their time with a little drinking, eating, talking, and watching. As someone so aptly said, "Aperitif time is when half of France watches the other half go by." I spent many a delightful hour sipping cocktails and watching the stylish Parisians stroll past.

Our first date was an enchanted evening. After our aperitifs we shared a delicious meal at the Night & Day Restaurant on the Champs-Elysées. Genevieve graciously declined my offer of wine, both during and after dinner. She was not a teetotaler, because she did drink on other occasions. I wondered if she sensed I wasn't much of a drinker and was looking out for me. She had a sense about things like that.

After dinner we took in a movie, *Bridge on the River Kwai*. I proposed a nightcap, which again was cordially refused. At the end of the evening I escorted her to her apartment via taxi, and we parted with a warm handshake. All those rumors one hears of how the French can drink like fish and make love at a snap of a finger were not true in my experience. Here was a beautiful, intelligent, and absolutely charming lady who didn't drink me under the table or allow us to rush into bed. We dated like this for months. And the more we dated, the more I got to know what true love and a good, happy relationship meant.

On weekdays I was busy with my entry-level GS-9 assignment as Dorm Counselor at the Paris American High School. Three colleagues and I were responsible for 160 teenagers in grades nine through twelve, from outlying bases that didn't have high schools. The students spent weekdays at the school and were bused home on the weekends. At night we really had to be on our toes to keep mischievous teenage boys and girls in their appropriate dorms, to prevent unauthorized co-ed rendezvous.

A tragic incident occurred one Friday afternoon when the bus was ready to leave. The army major chaperoning the bus asked us to wait while he went to the restroom. After some delay he finally boarded looking ghostly pale. He responded gruffly to our concerns about whether he was okay. After the bus went on its way, the janitor ran out of the boys bathroom in a panic, shouting that it looked like a murder happened in there. There was blood streaked all over the floor, and the sink looked as if someone had hurriedly tried to clean it up with paper towels. The Crime Investigation Department, or CID, investigated it as a possible crime scene. A rumor hinting at an illicit abortion started, although this didn't seem logical in a boy's bathroom. On the following Monday the news broke that the major had died late Friday night from a perforated intestine caused by ruptured stomach ulcers. Sadly, he may not have realized the gravity of his illness. This tragedy impacted me greatly, and it remains in my memory.

My weekends were filled with the courtship of Genevieve. That year brought us a whirlwind of romance as we met for movies, dancing, stage shows, and long, engaging conversations over dinner.

A year after our first date, and at the same Champs-Elysées restaurant, I held her hand in mine and asked her to marry me. She softly replied, "I'll think about it and let you know tomorrow." I didn't sleep a wink that night. The next day at lunch she looked in my eyes and smiled, saying, "Yes, Dan, I'll marry you." My heart leapt for joy. I was the luckiest man on earth.

Our city hall civil ceremony, preceding our church wedding. Christine, who no-showed to meet Genevieve for lunch the day we first met, is wearing a white hat.

We were married at the American Church in Paris on December 19th, 1959. We were both twenty-nine years old.

It's amazing how one small occurrence can change everything. If either of our friends had shown up for lunch on my first day in Paris, our lives would have been completely different. Instead, I had found my true love, and the future awaited us.

***

Genevieve was born in August of 1929 in the small village of Chatillon sur Seine, about 50 miles north of Dijon. Some of the finest vineyards in the world are found in the area, better known as Burgundy.

The Seine River literally flowed through the back yard of her family's home, and sometimes overflowed into the house. The Seine's source is only a few miles south of Chatillon, and it's amazing to see a trickle of water coming out of a hillside to meander through France and become a thousand-mile river, emptying into the Atlantic Ocean. What stories the river could tell, if it could speak of its rich history through the ages!

Genevieve was the third daughter in a family of four girls and a boy. Her father was a Spanish immigrant who established a prosperous farm machinery business, providing a comfortable

upper middle class lifestyle for his family in their 300-year old stone farmhouse. The rural community of Chatillon provided an idyllic childhood setting along the scenic Seine for Genevieve and her siblings to play at the river's shaded edge and ride bicycles along the country roads.

In 1940, Germany's WWII forces invaded and occupied France, sweeping across the country in a wave of death and destruction. French citizens, fleeing south towards Spain to escape the carnage of the German advance, used any transportation available to them. Cars, trucks, horse-drawn carts, and people on foot carrying suitcases crammed the roads as low-flying German planes bombed and strafed the columns of civilian vehicles. Genevieve's family of seven fled in their car with only enough time to grab a few of their most necessary belongings. The whole family dashed from the car into the ditches every time German aircraft appeared. Luckily they escaped the bombs and machine gun fire, but after the raids they returned to the road to see slumped bodies in bullet-riddled cars. Many of the dead were older people who couldn't move fast enough to get away. Genevieve, only eleven years old, remembered how men would push the cars off the road with the dead people in them.

Genevieve at age eighteen

Her family continued south and took temporary refuge in a house with others who had left the war-torn areas. During this time, Genevieve's father was stricken with cancer and his health was deteriorating. After the ceasefire, her family made the long trip back to Chatillon to find the town bombed to ruins. Surprisingly, their home and the machine shop were intact, but taken over by Germans. Genevieve's mother bravely begged the German commander to let them back into their home so she could care for her five children and dying husband, as they had nowhere else to go. The Germans allowed the family to stay, providing they agreed to feed the mechanics who were camped in the machine shop. These men entered the house unannounced at any hour to demand food and drink. The family had no source of income, and their home had been looted of any valuables. The children scoured the nearby countryside daily to find food and ask for help from farmers who knew their ailing father, who passed away within the year.

The Germans knew that many French citizens secretly provided food and supplies for members of the Resistance who fought to overcome the occupation. Suspecting her of aiding the Resistance, German soldiers threw a hand grenade in Genevieve's direction while driving past as she bicycled home from a nearby village with food for her family. The deafening explosion knocked her off the road and spattered her with shrapnel, but she managed to get back on her bike and rush home. Her mother spent hours pulling the bits of steel from her terrified daughter's cut and bleeding skin. Some tiny pieces couldn't be removed and migrated around in her body, with metal shards occasionally appearing decades later as bumps under her skin. When the metal bits moved about, she scratched at the itchy, irritated feeling. Throughout our married life these pieces came close to the surface, sometimes traveling across her face and lips, only to disappear and return again a few months later. We didn't think it caused any harm other than being an annoyance, and our doctors concurred.

Genevieve and her siblings continued with their school attendance through the German occupation. One day two Gestapo men in their black leather coats came into the classroom and asked for two students, a brother and sister, and took them away. After school Genevieve ran home and told her mother, who promptly went to their neighbor's house to find it empty. The parents, grandmother and two children were gone..taken away and never heard from or seen again. The family was Jewish.

The French people struggled to maintain normality with their lives during the wartime occupation, amid constant skirmishes between the Resistance and the Germans. In the summer of 1944 the French Resistance captured a German battalion commander in the Limousin region, to the southwest. In swift retaliation, a Nazi Das Reich SS command descended upon the nearby village of Oradour sur Glane and ordered its 640 occupants to assemble in the town square with their identification papers. The town's men were ordered to march to several barns, only to face deadly machine gun fire and then be incinerated along with the structures. The women and children were locked into the town's church which was then torched, and those who tried to escape were gunned down as they climbed out of the burning building. One woman climbed out of a rear window, took a bullet but dragged herself into the brush and was rescued the next day. She was the only survivor of the historic Oradour sur Glane Massacre. In a few hours a thousand-year old community was looted and bombed, and its occupants murdered horrifically. After the war, De Gaulle declared the town a permanent memorial to the cruelty of Nazi occupation, never to be rebuilt.

Following the infamous Battle of Normandy, additional Allied forces approached from the south to drive the Germans out of France. In the fall of 1944, Genevieve's family heard a great deal of shooting and her mother closed all the shutters as everyone got down on the floor. When it was over, they cautiously went outside to find American and British troops and tanks rumbling through town. Jubilant citizens ran alongside the jeeps and tanks, with children climbing aboard to ride in the makeshift parade. We still have the news photo of 16-year old Genevieve riding high on a jeep among the celebratory crowd on the day of liberation. The Americans also brought chocolate and gum, treats the French children hadn't seen in years. Genevieve's mother had remarried the previous year, around the time Genevieve entered high school. The post-war cleanup effort went into full swing and things were returning to normal.

Genevieve's high school Latin teacher, an amateur archaeologist, had been ex-cavating a site near Chatillon when he discovered the ancient tomb of a woman of Greek aristocracy, dating from 500 B.C. The class was told that their teacher had made a great discovery and would not be at school for a few days. He had been studying the Vix Grave site for years before uncovering the largest known ancient metal vessel; the Vase de Vix. Hammered from a single sheet of bronze, after restoration it stands 64" tall, holds 290 gallons, and features motifs of horse-drawn chariots along the top edge. The beautiful bronze relic and other findings from the tomb are on display in the museum at Chatillon.

Genevieve's education continued in the local school where she majored in Latin language and excelled in all her courses. With her extraordinary linguistic ability, she also mastered English, Italian, Spanish, German, and eventually Arabic and Japanese. She was well qualified for her position as a translator for the U.S. Army offices in Paris, where I met her in 1958, within a day of my arrival.

***

With marriage I also became a parent. Genevieve's son Eric, by her previous marriage, was a perky five-year old, handsome and intelligent, as adorable as Genevieve herself. He was full of life, energy, and curiosity, and he enriched my life in so many ways. At first, he didn't speak English, nor did I speak French, but we managed to communicate. Without hesitation I accepted him as my son, and he accepted me as his father. I wouldn't have had it any other way. One of my colleagues on my next assignment

Five year-old Eric took this photo of us with my camera on our first day of marriage

in Verona, Italy had introduced one of her children as her son and her other child as her stepson. I'll never forget the feeling of seeing that boy's downcast face. I realized at that moment that I would always introduce Eric as my son and think of him as my own. It has been so ever since.

In fact, Eric came with Genevieve and me on our honeymoon. He was living with his grandparents at their farm in Chatillon, and we stopped there to visit with my new in-laws before going to Italy. The plan had been for Eric to remain with them for another six months while I settled into my new assignment as a fourth-grade teacher in Verona. As we said our farewells, Genevieve, a devoted mother, turned to me and gently asked, "Dan, can't we take Eric with us now? This way we can start our new life together." I couldn't refuse my beautiful bride, and it turned out to be one of the best decisions we made. She always knew the right thing to do.

Our tiny compact Dauphine was crammed to the roof with our belongings. We somehow squeezed a small bag for Eric in the car, but with no unused space Eric rode on his mother's lap...the entire 700-kilometer journey!

I had rented a second-floor apartment for us in advance of our arrival. It was small but adequate, with a furnished living room, dining room, bath, and two bedrooms. Not expecting Eric to join us so soon, I had piled his room with a clutter of borrowed pots, pans, kitchenware and dishes stacked on the bed to be put away. When we arrived, he ran excitedly into his new bedroom, looked at the mess, and said something in French to his mother. I never learned what he had said, but Genevieve chuckled warmly.

Life in Verona was busy but idyllic. We enrolled Eric in first grade at the American Elementary School for military dependents, where I was teaching fourth grade. Within four months he was speaking both English and Italian. It was remarkable.

Genevieve, as well as Eric, quickly learned Italian, and we made many Italian friends. Genevieve also had the benefit of being part of the large French community in the area.

On my $4,000 annual salary we lived from one paycheck to the next, but we managed. The government was good to its employees. In addition to covering some of our living expenses, we enjoyed recreational facilities on Lake Garda and had free use of ski equipment on the winter slopes. The government's benefits contributed greatly to our comfort and security, especially in the early years of our marriage.

In Verona we were just a day's drive away from my relatives in the sunny southern part of the country. Although my grandparents on both sides of my family had passed away years earlier, my cousins, aunts and uncles still lived in the villages from where my grandparents had come. I was excited to see them and to introduce them to Genevieve and Eric, but I knew their rural lifestyle was unsophisticated. It certainly didn't include the conveniences we take for granted. During Easter vacation four months after our wedding, it was time, and we headed first to Montesano, in Calabria. My Italian relatives didn't have telephones so I had written to them during the holidays saying we'd be there, but I wasn't sure yet of the dates.

In Montesano, a small, hilltop town, the cobbled lanes were too narrow for cars, so we parked by the church. Everyone knew each other, so we only needed to inquire of the Cardinale family to be directed to the home of my mother's older sister Sarah and her ailing elderly husband.

The stucco house had paned windows, a bare stone floor, and no indoor heating or plumbing. In early spring the night air was chilly, so we warmed ourselves around a copper cauldron filled with hot coals from the wood-burning stove in the kitchen. Water was available to the homes via pipes along the street. Residents filled buckets at the spigot and carried them indoors for cooking and washing. We washed ourselves in an enameled washbasin and then poured the used water into the kitchen sink that drained into the street gutter, eventually flowing to creeks and brush below. Electricity was also very basic. Only a bare bulb hung from the ceiling of each room. When we asked about using the toilet, Aunt Sarah led us to the cellar stairway, handed us a shovel, and pointed to the dirt floor, instructing us to do our business there and bury it. Surprisingly, there was no offensive smell emanating from the basement. If Genevieve was shocked or surprised by the primitive bathroom facilities, she never let on. She was gracious, as always.

That night Genevieve, Eric, and I shared the bedroom where my mother had been born in 1902. After breakfast the next day we drove several hundred miles farther south to the "boot" of Italy, where my dad was born in the Calabria countryside. Upon reaching the seaside town of Amantea in the late afternoon, we stopped at a rustic farmhouse and asked for directions to find my aunt and cousins. Eric took one look at the place and queried, "Can we stay at a hotel, Daddy?"

We continued on until only scattered farms were visible from the road. Parking at the base of a hill, we hiked up the steep, narrow road past twisted old fig and olive trees. I was filled with sadness when we walked by the farmhouse where Dad was born. My father's relatives had moved up the hill to another structure on the same property. Apparently they had sold the house out of financial necessity, because their current residence appeared to have once been the farm's meat-curing shed. Knocking on the rough-planked door, I thought, "But for the grace of God, I would be living here," giving silent thanks that my parents had both sought a different life for themselves.

My dad's brother Ventura and his wife, also named Sarah, greeted us with gracious country hospitality. Their house can only be described as basic shelter. It had no electricity and no plumbing. When I say "no plumbing," I mean that there was no indoor plumbing of any kind, not even an outhouse. The facilities were anywhere outdoors on the hillside, such as in the bushes or behind a rock. The windows had no glass or screens; they were simply square holes in the walls that were always wide open. Chickens

An old, termite-holed postcard showing the view from my father's family farm.

roosted in the sills at night, facing into the rooms as their droppings decorated the outside wall. And so it was in the room where we slept. On the other side of our bed, long strings of homemade sausages draped over broomsticks hung horizontally from the ceiling. Sausage grease dripped onto the packed dirt floor.

Genevieve did not comment or complain about these accommodations; not even the bathroom facilities. I have often wondered what impression this gave her of my family in the States, whom she hadn't yet met. If she worried about what she had gotten herself into by marrying me, she never mentioned it.

In this impoverished region of Italy, the people spoke a Calabrese dialect. I was able to communicate with my uncle and aunt, but Genevieve's school-learned Veronese or "northern" Italian was quite different and required me to translate for her.

Dinner was also a different experience for us. After serving a chicken dinner, my aunt and female cousins began to leave the room. I was confused and asked Aunt Sarah to sit and dine with us, but she shook her head, explaining, "No, no, no! The men eat first." I realized this was their custom, but it felt terribly unfair. At their insistence, Genevieve, as she was a guest, and I ate with the men. Once they had their fill, the women ate what was left over.

The traditional domestic roles of men and women in Calabria were strikingly different than my upbringing in the U.S. Here, the men spent their time shooting any birds, including crows, that happened to fly over. They also fished in the Mediterranean from the rocks. Other than these two activities, the men were very good at eating. The women did absolutely everything else. Women's work included cleaning and cooking fish and game, tending the livestock of chickens, rabbits, and sheep, baking fresh bread, picking and drying figs, making sausage, and canning vegetables. They wore large, food-stained aprons and filled them with the figs they gathered. The young women, always barefoot, carried spring water on a steep dirt path up the hill to the farm shacks, balancing a water jug on a rolled cloth on their heads while carrying another full heavy jug under each arm. We felt as though we'd gone back in time. Except for our clothing, we might have been in the Middle Ages.

The next day we awoke to a beautiful morning. When Eric ran outside to explore he found two new friends around his age that he could communicate with in Italian. Together they roamed the hillside playing with friendly dogs, climbing boulders and olive

Eric exploring an Amantea hillside.

trees, and chasing sheep and ducks. Eric was having the time of his life, and now he never wanted to leave!

From the slopes of the farm we took in breathtaking views of the Mediterranean with Sicily on the horizon. Some of my uncles, aunts and cousins had tried living in the U.S. for a time, but they returned to their ancestral homes and lived happily. Conversely, Mother never had any desire to go back to Italy, not even for a visit, and Dad wanted to see his home country and relatives again, but never made the trip.

On other occasions while exploring Italy we sometimes visited my country relatives, bringing them gifts of chocolate and cigarettes from the PX. But there were no more sleepovers among the chickens and sausages.

* * *

Back in Verona, I was happy beyond belief, but my newfound family soon faced its first crisis together. Following Genevieve and Eric's visit to her parents in Chatillon during summer vacation, Eric went to stay with his biological father. When it was time to return home, Genevieve wired me in distress saying that

Eric's father not only refused to give him back, but had enrolled him in a local school! It appeared Eric's father intended to keep him permanently.

I was 700 kilometers away, but I immediately took off, driving the entire distance to France in less than twenty-four hours. After I picked up Genevieve we headed for Dijon and spoke with lawyers to determine our custody rights. I found them completely unsympathetic to an American, as French law favors the biological father. While driving through Dijon, we began a heated argument on how to proceed.

Genevieve, the cautious and patient one, was willing to follow due process through the courts and wait it out. This was a sensible approach, but it would have taken months. I wanted action now. My method was very direct. I would go to his father's home or the school, and just pick up Eric and take off. With both of us under extreme emotional stress, resisting any sort of compromise, our quarrel intensified and reached the breaking point. When the car came to a stop she suddenly bolted, firmly ending our heated disagreement. "Go back to Italy!" she demanded, "I'll handle this. I'll wait it out and get Eric back." And she took off!

Regretfully, I let her go. In matters of the heart, painful emotions interfere with rational thinking. We were now too angry and hurt for further discussion. In dazed disbelief, I turned the car back in the direction of Italy.

I drove for some distance when I realized that I was passing through the town where Eric might be attending school. I decided that I wasn't going back without trying. It was raining, as I nervously took my chances and approached the school.

A wet mist engulfed the entire area. I pulled up in front of the school behind the noontime bus that takes students home for lunch. Waiting with the engine running, an eternity passed between each sweep of the wipers. My thoughts raced, my heart pounded, and my anxiety grew. Will I see him? Will he see me? Is this the bus he boards? I felt helpless. I hoped and prayed that I wouldn't miss him in the rain. I was so fiercely determined, I resolved that if Eric boarded the bus I would flag it down to take him off.

Then he was there! With each swipe of the wipers, he would fade into the rain and then reappear. To my utter amazement, he was coming straight towards the car. It was unbelievable! He didn't know I would be there. He didn't even know I was in the country. As I leaned over and opened the door, his first words were, "Hi, Daddy. Where's Mama?" I didn't answer him directly, responding, "Let's go, Son, and we'll join her." By simply opening the car door, I now had Eric safely with me, without any lawyers or paperwork or courtroom testimony. My fears and apprehensions vanished momentarily, but then my thoughts turned to Genevieve. Where was she? What was she doing? Was she okay? How foolish of me to let her go. Yet, if not for our argument and her demand that I go home, I wouldn't have been there at exactly the right moment to find Eric. What a gamble I had made, and it worked!

I sped out of the village. At a junction in the highway I could have proceeded straight to Eric's father's house. Instead, I took a quick right turn towards Chatillon. "Are we going to get my clothes?" Eric calmly asked, either sensing or knowing what was happening.

My emotions imploded all at once, and tears rolled down my face. Eric, so young and innocent, asked, "Why are you crying, Daddy? Aren't you happy?" I felt relieved and grateful, and I told him my tears were for Mother, who would be so very happy to see him. My heart ached as I thought of Genevieve and our hurtful argument. I had caused her such terrible distress.

The drizzle became a downpour, and we needed to find her. As I drove on, Eric curled up next to me and fell asleep. My eyes kept welling up with tears as I thought of Genevieve. I knew I was in a race against time to find her and leave the country as soon as possible. The police were surely alerted by now and looking for the missing boy.

Although I thought Genevieve was likely headed back to her parents, I stopped first at the home of her friend in Dijon to ask if Genevieve had been there. By invitation, Eric and I waited inside for a time. When she didn't show up, I thanked the friend and continued on to Chatillon, taking the chance that the most obvious place would be the least likely place the authorities would look. As a precaution, I parked the car some distance from her parent's house. I even made a false license plate, preparing to use it if someone recognized and reported the car.

In Chatillon I explained the day's events to Genevieve's parents, who, of course, became very concerned. It was now after dark and still raining. She'd been gone for almost six hours. I paced the parlor floor, my mind churning. Where was she? Could she be hurt? Was she in danger? I began to worry that in bringing back my son, I may have lost my wife. How could good intentions go so terribly wrong?

We waited for the knock on the door that would either tell us Genevieve had come home or the police had come for Eric. On several occasions there were false alarms, with some other person stopping by. At every noise or knock, Eric ran to hide and my heart leaped in my chest.

And then the knock for which we had been waiting. There stood Genevieve, soaking wet, shivering, and tearful, as Eric dashed into her open arms. All our differences were instantly dissolved. With tears of joy, we embraced.

Genevieve told us that as she walked for those six hours in the rain, she somehow knew Eric would be with me, in spite of the great odds against us. In her heart she held onto the belief that Eric was safely in my care.

It was imperative for us to move fast. We contacted our lawyer, who, in turn, informed Eric's father that the boy was safe and well. We learned that when Eric wasn't on the bus, his father had called the school, and officials had given him a description of our car. Luckily, the rain had obscured our car's Italian license plates from the army base, so they were mistaken for Belgian plates. It was one small factor that worked in our favor.

Once again united as a family, the three of us started on the long road back to Italy. Apprehensively, we neared the Italian border. We had no idea what might await us there. If Eric's father, assuming we had quickly left the country, had not alerted the authorities, we wouldn't have any problems. If he suspected Eric was still in French jurisdiction, however, we could be in trouble.

My palms were sweaty as we waited in line behind other cars, and I pulled forward hesitantly to hand the border guard our passports. He methodically opened each book, looked at the pictures, looked at us, and then at the pictures again. Neither Genevieve nor I were breathing. He ordered us to wait and went into his guard shack, as our hearts thumped and our throats went dry. I had the car running and in gear, with the foolish thought of fleeing if necessary. After a few eternal seconds, the guard came back. With a "Merci, avanti, avanti," he waved us across the border. I checked the rearview mirror to ensure that the border guard wasn't chasing us with guns drawn, and heaved a sigh of relief.

Eric's father never gave us any real problems after that. He accepted the fact that Eric wouldn't return to live with him. Through our lawyer we mutually agreed on visiting rights. Eric treated me as his real father, and we got along beautifully as a father and son team. We had the kind of love and understanding that could only be ideal between a parent and child.

***

With our family crisis resolved, we settled down to our daily life, delighted to be immersed in Verona's rich history, culture, and arts. Every tourist who comes to Italy should visit this romantic city of Shakespeare's Romeo and Juliet with its fountains, towers, statues, and piazzas. We loved all the sights and experiences it had to offer, such as the majestic arched stone bridges spanning the scenic Adige River. Dating back as far as 100 B.C., they are a central feature of the city. We attended performances at the

Verona Arena, a beautifully intact Roman-built outdoor amphi-
theater with perfect natural acoustics, where lavish operas are
presented for up to 30,000 spectators. We also found time for
weekend snow skiing, as well as swimming and water skiing at
Lake Garda, sometimes on the same day, as the mountains were
not far away. Adapting to our new environment, Eric and Genevieve learned to speak Italian; and as for me, I improved somewhat but could not shake my ear-bending southern Calabrese
dialect.

In Verona I began my model train hobby. I had originally
bought a set for Eric. He played with it, but I must admit, I played
with it more. I kept adding to it at every base where I was assigned, and it grew into a huge and elaborate set.

I kept very busy teaching between thirty and thirty-eight
fourth graders, at any given time. I was responsible for all in-
struction, except music and Italian language. In those days we
did not have curriculum guides to follow, nor were there teaching specialists to check on us. Textbooks were provided, but it
was up to each teacher to decide how to present the material. In
particular, I loved teaching science and art, and I initiated new
programs for which I received awards. As an example, I taught
the students how to build a homemade telescope and organized
evenings of stargazing to view the moon's craters, Saturn's rings,
and the bright colors of Mars. To supplement the astronomy lesson, we hung a model of the solar system from the ceiling on
strings. Another science lesson involved assembling electrical cir-
cuits with flashing lights that ran on batteries on a large wooden
easel board, a rough fabricated precursor to the computer age.

In my classroom we had a mini-zoo of guinea pigs, hamsters
(a new generation came along every twenty-eight days), and a
pregnant rabbit that gave us a litter of twelve to fifteen babies.
When the animals were large enough, the children took them
home for a week and learned to take care of them. To go along
with the live animals we used paper mache and chicken wire to
create eight-to-ten feet tall creatures, including elephants and

bears. Our Smokey the Bear was so realistic it once frightened the night watchman. Our giant, paper mache giraffe was a celebrity in Verona's annual Mardi Gras parade. We set it on a cart and my class pulled it along, as we handed out bubble gum to the young bystanders.

For art class, my students crafted colorful puppets and wrote puppet-plays that they performed for the other classes. We built a large fake fireplace where the children pretended to burn trashy words they had said or heard. I believed these various exercises helped children to learn.

All my students were eager and well behaved, and I still recall many of their names and faces. One such student was Michael St. Savor, a shy boy whose social skills blossomed in a creative atmosphere. Another was David Romano, a brilliant student who needed challenge to keep him motivated. The children's enthusiasm motivated me to keep dreaming up more activities, and the time flew by. The parents of several students related noticeable improvements in their children's behavior at home, validating my efforts.

I dedicated many evening hours to planning and organizing overnight camping trips, Boy Scout troop hikes, and Saturday art classes. Genevieve never complained about the time I spent away from home on extracurricular activities. Many years later she confided how she had cried with loneliness while I was out working late, and it became painfully clear that my obsessive dedication to teaching had caused me to be neglectful of her feelings.

Verona Elementary School was housed in a converted shoe factory. The doors and windows leaked, even after the Army attempted repairs. When I complained to the principal, he said he couldn't do anything more about it. I found the conditions intolerable, and I came up with my own solution. Learning about the Government Suggestion Program, I submitted my idea on the applicable DoD form, personally delivered it the appropriate committee, and received, amazingly, permission to proceed. After the work was completed, the general in charge presented me with a certificate and a letter to my principal. I was pleased that the system worked, although it took some time and effort.

At the end of our third year in Verona, my principal, Phil Harr, suggested I pursue a promotion in administration with better pay and further opportunities for advancement. Genevieve was always supportive of my career goals, and she agreed that I apply. As a result I was selected to head up a school at Braconne, near the city of Angouleme in southwest France, to begin the phase of my career I refer to as "Climbing the Ladder" of success.

FOUR

Climbing the Ladder

BRACONNE, FRANCE

We were very fortunate to move from one beautiful city to another. My job assignment after Verona took us to the ancient city of Angouleme, in southwest France. We rented a charming apartment in a building rooted on thirty-foot thick hillside ramparts constructed in the Middle Ages to defend against invasions during the religious wars. Old chestnut trees shaded the building's entrance, and our windows overlooked a magnificent medieval cathedral. We enjoyed fresh produce from the nearby Saturday farmer's market, and the center of town and famous Hotel de Ville were a ten-minute walk from our door.

The U.S. Army base of Braconne, where I started my first GS-10 position as elementary school principal, was a convenient ten-minute drive. The mission of this base was to store backup supplies for postwar U.S. bases in Germany, which could be quickly transported eastward if hostilities heightened with Russia. The base storage facilities were unbelievably enormous. Crated equipment and army vehicles were kept outdoors, safely covered under the trees on thousands of wooded acres in the huge forest of Braconne.

News of our arrival in Angouleme brought a dinner invitation from the president of the Franco-American Club's local chapter. We spent many an evening visiting in our respective homes with Dr. Gavel and his lovely wife Jackie, who became our lifelong friends. During the war Dr. Gavel had been a member of the Marquis, or the French Resistance. He told riveting stories of daily tragedies and victories fighting the Germans on French soil. The Franco-American Club held their annual meetings at our school's auditorium. On these occasions they remembered the fallen who had been captured, tortured, and killed, and they celebrated life with a sumptuous banquet of roasted lamb. The men and women of the Marquis were brave and selfless people.

Genevieve was happy to be back in her home country again. Seeking some form of exercise to keep active, she inquired about fencing lessons at a local club. As it was closed that day, she went to inquire at the horseback riding club. Genevieve confessed her fear of horses to the club's owner, an experienced horseman. He produced his gentlest horse for Genevieve to pat on the neck, and my wife's love of horses began.

Genevieve competing in an equestrian event

She borrowed a well-trained horse for her daily riding lessons, and after six months entered their first dressage competition and won a ribbon! Genevieve and this graceful animal were perfectly paired. Over the next three years together they won prize money, ribbons, and cups competing in steeplechase, cross-country, and jumping. Genevieve donated the prize money back to the club, but we kept the silver trophies, and at one point we had sixteen of them! Eric and I attended her events and were bursting with pride at her accomplishments.

On one occasion Eric went on a forest ride with a group, but when they arrived back at the stables, Eric's horse was trailing along in the back...but without Eric! How could a group of riders not notice when an eight-year old went missing in the deep forest? Our minds raced with all kinds of accidents that could happen with a horse and rider. Frantically, we sent out two search parties...one by car, and the other by horse. We drove up the road to the point where the trail exited the forest and began calling out for him, and there was Eric walking towards us, without a concern in the world! I grabbed him up in my arms and asked if he'd been hurt. "No, I'm okay," he said, "I did fall off my horse and he got away so I followed the trail here. I pretended I was a cowboy shot off my horse, and it was fun!" Apparently the horse spooked and Eric went flying, but thank goodness he wasn't hurt. I was miffed at the adults on the ride for not paying more attention, but with all ending well, I kept it to myself.

Genevieve was training a friend's horse to jump over obstacles when she took a fall. The friend brought her home and with pain in her voice Genevieve said, "Dan, I think I broke something and you'd better take me to the hospital." An X-ray showed a dislocated shoulder, and this was two days before we were to leave for a visit to the States. It didn't appear that we'd make the trip, but our dear friend Dr. Gavel put her shoulder back into joint and made a brace for her to wear.

We took off by train to Paris with an overnight stay there, then boarded the long flight from Paris to New York. Fortunately my sister Jean picked us up at LaGuardia and we didn't have to fly into Newark, because we were exhausted. For the next two months we remained stateside and Genevieve was in varying amounts of pain the entire time, though she never complained. A few weeks after we returned to France, she was back to jumping horses again.

During my term at Braconne, the oral-dose form of Polio vaccine had just become available and we administered the vaccine to all the children by putting a few drops on sugar cubes. Everyone took their dose willingly because polio was a terrible crippling disease, which had reached epidemic proportions in the U.S. during the 1940s and 50s. Dr. Jonas Salk, of my home state, Pennsylvania, had developed this highly successful vaccine.

A challenge in my administration job was dealing with the annual exodus of teaching staff who transferred out after only one school year because they wanted to work in the bigger schools of Paris and Italy. These American teachers had sought European assignments to be near the world-famous metropolitan areas. Our school was somewhat of a whistle-stop for teachers, although I certainly empathized with their sense of adventure. How fortunate I was to have had Paris as my first assignment, as I had launched my new life and fallen in love there, all in the same day!

The Braconne base commander was Colonel Kiley, a wonderful person beloved by all. He always supported us for our endeavors, and the base officers, enlisted personnel, and civilian workers appreciated his leadership. When he received orders to transfer to another base, the officers organized a going-away party, and what a bash it was! The liquor flowed and the revelry went into the night. Well, it just happened that one of our art projects at the school was to build an eight-foot tall paper mache elephant, and several of the other teachers and I prepared a surprise for the evening's festivities. We painted the elephant pink and wrote "Bon voyage Col. Kiley" on its side. We then arranged for a truck and ladder to be available on the night of the celebration. Slipping away from the party undetected, we attached the pink elephant to the chimney of Col. Kiley's house. The next day the commander called to say, "All that partying paid off, because I really did see pink elephants!"

Braconne's on-base officers' club hosted a very popular "Franco-American Night" event regularly. During one of these meetings we received the unbelievable announcement that President Kennedy had been shot. Several embassy officials in attendance at our gathering left immediately for their consulate in Bordeaux, and the rest of us stayed up all night listening to the news. Many French and American tears were shed. The next day when eight-year old Eric heard the news, he cried, too. For days to follow, our numerous French friends stopped by the house to express their sincere condolences at the tragic loss of our country's much-admired leader. The French people adored President Kennedy.

I had a great school with excellent teachers, good command support, a lovely apartment, and Genevieve, a natural on a horse, was at her height in Concours hippiques. Life was good and I would have stayed, but I wanted to provide well for my family and excel in educating young people, so I never turned down a promotion. The DoDDS administration office offered me the GS-11 principal position at Chateauroux Air Base Elementary School, twice as large as my present school. I took the offer and we moved, leaving behind good friends and fond memories.

CHATEAUROUX

It was 1965, and we arrived at Chateauroux Air Base and found an apartment on the eleventh floor of the only skyscraper in town. It looked out of place surrounded by the smaller and more typical French apartment buildings and homes, but the location was great. The Chateauroux base was part of NATO, so we had many diverse nationalities living in the building. There were Swedes, Turks, Germans, Italians, French, Belgians, Dutch, English, and more. At mealtime, tempting fragrances of exotic cuisine mingled in the hallways and beckoned to the senses.

Genevieve joined a riding club in the area and soon she was jumping horses and winning more cups and ribbons. But no sport is without its risks. One day I came home to find her sitting in a chair with one leg swollen to twice its normal size from her ankle to above the knee, and in frightening hues of red, blue, and purple. She had borrowed a good riding horse with a known reputation, and the moment Genevieve let down her guard, that horse planted a solid kick on her leg. With rest and good care she recovered and went back to her regular activities. I was confident in her abilities, but privately, I sometimes worried about her safety with these powerful and sometimes unpredictable animals.

Through some of our new French friends, we heard about a snow-skiing class credit program for fifth and sixth grade students. We enrolled a number of our on-base American students, and it was a fabulous experience for everyone. The program consisted of a two-week stay at a ski resort in the French Alps, with regular school class in the mornings and ski lessons in the afternoons. Genevieve was a skilled skier and assisted in the program along with several teachers and parents. Our school continued its participation in the program for the next few years and the students gained great value from it.

In a small village near Chateauroux, an annual festival was held to give high honor to the lowly snail. As the story goes, the Roman Army was saved by the humble escargot. Almost two thousand years earlier, the Romans marched through this locale on their way to what is now Britain, but faced starvation after expending all their food supplies. The general ordered the cooks to scour the surrounding land for something which could feed an army, but all they could find were snails... millions of them! The cooks boiled the snails, mixed them with herbs, garlic, and salt, and there you have it. The mayor of this tiny village established a celebration for the discovery that "saved the Roman Army." The day of feasting included a parade with marching bands, and a king and queen of the escargots. The villagers served up heaping trays of three dozen escargots with French bread and a bottle of wine for the equivalent of $8. These days, a half dozen of these tasty little mollusks will cost you twenty dollars in some restaurants. For me, it was love at first bite when I first tried them after arriving in Paris. In time, I became a bona fide connoisseur of escargots.

LAON AIR BASE

Following our wonderful year in Chateauroux, I accepted a promotion to Laon Air Base in northern France. I was principal of both Laon Elementary and Junior High, but the two school facilities were located on opposite sides of the base. Sparing ourselves an inconvenient commute, the assistant principal and I agreed to split up the school year while he ran one school and I ran the other, then we'd switch. It was an odd but workable arrangement.

The principal who preceded me had ordered and taken delivery of sixty thousand dollars worth of musical instruments for the school, but when I arrived, no music teacher had been hired and no class space had been allocated. This was a typical example of wastefulness in the military, which just tore at my heart. The beautiful shiny instruments were turned over to a surplus store as salvage, and savvy military dependents were circling like vultures! They'd heard the rumors and followed the truck to where it was unloaded, lining up to pay pennies on the dollar. All the instruments were sold in one day. It was shocking to me to be part of a system that would spend all that money on valuable instruments and then send them away to be liquidated.

Laon was a fighter aircraft base, and its very busy runway happened to be only one hundred feet from the school. The jets roared off into the sky and then roared back in for a landing, all day long. In the classrooms and offices we had to stop talking and wait a minute until we could hear again.

The view from our apartment in Laon looked out towards the city's proud landmark, the twelfth-century Laon Cathedral with its distinctive gothic spires and life-size statues of oxen standing regally in its towers. The historic cathedral's stone building blocks were transported by these sturdy beasts, pulling heavily laden carts from quarries in the valley below. Legends tell of an ox-cart driver whose lead animal was ready to collapse with exhaustion, so the driver unhitched the tired ox to allow it some rest. The cart could not go on without its best ox, and the driver prayed for help. Just then another strong ox mysteriously appeared from the forest and stood eagerly waiting to pull the yoke. The driver hitched it to his cart and continued on to deliver the stones. Returning down the same road he found his old ox refreshed, so he released the replacement animal to return to the forest. It was never seen again. The enigmatic ox is known in stories as "The Ox that Helped." To honor their hard labor, the many oxen that helped build the cathedral were memorialized in stone.

I was captivated with the hobby of a very clever local jeweler-watchmaker, who had never been to America but held a fascination with American locomotives. He photographed catalog copies of American trains in order to create hand-built replicas in intricate detail. An expert machinist, he sketched all the working parts from his photos and fabricated to-scale smoke-stacks, train cars, and gears that turned the wheels. The toy trains, complete with working engines, tracks, depots and villages, were mounted on a large flat board attached to pulleys and hoisted up to the ceiling. To display and enjoy his trains, he would move all the furniture aside and lower the entire set down from above. Genevieve enjoyed our visits with this talented Frenchman as much as I did, and translated his answers to my many eager questions, as well as my descriptions of the trains I'd worked with in my early college days in Hoboken.

ORLEANS ARMY BASE

I transferred to Orleans base as principal for the on-base elementary and junior high schools. Orleans served as the U.S. Army headquarters in France, and was the last of our military bases in the country. President De Gaulle was a powerful and innovative leader, and by his orders the U.S. shut down all its bases and pulled operations out of France within a few years. My former DoDDS assignments in Paris, Braconne, and Laon had all been closed by then, in 1967. Other closed bases included Fontainebleau, Croix Chapeau, Evreux, Metz, and Dreux.

We lived off base in the city center of Orleans, in walking distance to churches, restaurants, and markets. Eric was enrolled in a local French school and Genevieve found another excellent equestrian facility where she rode and competed. Orleans is the entrance to the Loire Valley, known as "The Valley of Kings and Queens." With many well-preserved and breathtaking chateaus within a day's driving distance, Orleans is ideally situated to explore the Loire.

Heading up another great school filled with 600 students and thirty competent teachers, I was happy at my job. One teacher was particularly unforgettable. Our sixth grade teacher, John Egan, was stationed on the U.S.S. Arizona when Japan bombed Pearl Harbor, and he described the attack as "Hell on Earth." John was outside on deck in the early morning of December 7th when Japanese aircraft filled the sky and bombs exploded through the steel battleship, killing over a thousand crewmen and officers who were trapped below. He was among the fortunate few who were able to dive off the ship. "The bombs and explosions were deafening, even from under water. When I came up for air, a thick layer of oil covered the water," he told me, "and my first thought was of all that oil catching fire." Swimming through the oil and away from the ship, John was picked up by a rubber dinghy with other shocked and injured survivors on board. "As we headed towards shore, I saw bodies floating and men dying. These were my shipmates, my buddies. It was horrific." Soon after the little rescue boat reached safety, the oil slick did catch fire. Pearl Harbor was ablaze, black smoke billowed skyward, sirens blared, and majestic battleships were smoldering on their sides, still at their moorings.

After the war, John married a lovely Englishwoman and they had adorable twin girls. As a teacher, he was dynamic and enthusiastic. He loved to make the children laugh. His pranks and sense of humor kept us all entertained, although it backfired on him once during a visit from some distinguished guests from the French school system. I offered them an impromptu tour of the school, and after seeing several other classrooms, I told the VIPs how much I wanted them to meet a very outstanding educator. We went into John's classroom but he'd stepped out. After a momentary wait, suddenly John flew in the door yelling "SU-PER-MAN!" while holding his blue blazer jacket like a cape. John froze in his steps, looked at all the unexpected adults in the room, and you could have heard a pin drop.

I was given orders to tell John to shave off his beard, which the army didn't allow on base. Hesitantly, I explained that I was only the messenger, but rules are rules. "They can't tell me what to do with my face!" he stubbornly replied. I remained calm and asked him to please save us a lot of fuss by losing the fuzz. The next day he came into my office to briefly tell me something, and then stood looking at me. "Do you notice anything different?" he demanded. I didn't. John, almost shouting, said "You (so-and-so), I shaved and you didn't even notice, so what was the point of shaving it, anyway?"

My work was never boring. On another occasion the school nurse entered my office very upset, saying, "There's water shooting into my office from a hole in the wall!" The boys' restroom was on the other side of her wall, and I knew some construction work was being done, so we went to have a look. To our complete surprise, we found a boy urinating through the hole where the plumbers had drilled to add a new pipe. She nabbed him and told him he'd better have a good explanation for his behavior. "I was just practicing my aim," he said. I bit my lip to keep from laughing at this amusing boyish behavior while sternly warning him not to do it again.

The city of Orleans is sometimes called "The city of Joan of Arc." It's said that she saved the city, and regal statues of the warrior-heroine are found in many parks and public places. Every August, Joan of Arc Day is celebrated and faux fires flicker in the night, with red lights flashing in the cathedral windows and around the city to represent the flaming conclusion to the martyr's life.

Genevieve and I returned to Chateauroux AFB by special invitation for the closing party at the officer's club. The officers and fighter pilots really knew how to throw a party! Toward the end of the evening, the pilots decided they didn't want to leave anything intact for de Gaulle, who had requested our departure from France. They got rather carried away and tore the place apart. As if on a rampage, they broke everything that could be broken: chairs, tables, glassware, and dishes. We had enjoyed the party but didn't care for the destruction. Nevertheless, we thought these pilots should be given some slack. They would have given their lives to defend France from Russia, if an attack had occurred.

The last U.S. base to close was Orleans. It was sad to see the families and children leave, and we knew we would also miss our French friends. For the most part, I believe the French appreciated the U.S., especially after our troops liberated their country from Germany's occupation. There was no base closing party at Orleans, just people saying their goodbyes and busy packing to move to their next assignment, with many of them heading to our bases in West Germany.

I had the summer off before school was to start again in August, so we spent the time visiting Genevieve's family and enjoying some other sights in Europe before moving to my next job assignment.

FIVE

Libya and the Music Box

Genevieve had always dreamed of North Africa: its scenic desert, impressive date palms, and verdant oases. She found it all on my next assignment in Libya, a beautiful country in countless ways. Lovely gardens along the highway led to downtown Tripoli. The Arabs with their camel caravans traveling across the desert in the sun were romantically picturesque. In the nearly three years we lived there, we toured throughout the country to visit the northern coast and the interior, and we took trips to the desert. Libya was a fascinating place with wonderful people.

I was the GS-12 supervising principal in the school system at Wheelus Air Base with some fifteen hundred kindergarten through twelfth grade students. The school grounds had originally served as the stables and barracks for Mussolini's soldiers. The huge central courtyard was graced with ancient olive trees. There we built a "zoo," with goats, chickens, two camels, and a donkey. It was very educational for the children to interact with the animals and for me, as well, learning more about camels than I really wanted to know. Our school's young camels had become infested with ticks. When the ticks became bloated with blood, they hung from the camels' bellies like purple grapes. The Libyans told us the remedy: submerge the camels in the ocean, as the salt water would kill the ticks. The school was only a few blocks from the beautiful, clear, blue Mediterranean, so several of us led the camels to the shore, pushing and dragging them into the water as they cried and moaned pitifully in protest. These "ships of the desert" hate being in water, but after a few salt-water treatments the camels remained tick-free.

Genevieve fraternizing with one of our school's young camels

We were welcomed into the social circuit and mingled with interesting and well-traveled people both on and off the base: United Nations representatives, ambassadors, and relatives to the royal family. Horses played an important part in our life in Libya. Many of the ambassadors had their own horses, and friendships developed around the sport of riding and caring for these noble animals. Genevieve participated in the first equestrian jumping contest ever held in Libya. She took second place, and an Englishwoman came in first. The Libyan men were somewhat deflated as they placed third and fourth.

Genevieve studied Arabic. Able to communicate quite effectively, she was popular with the Libyans. She gave riding lessons to the children of the retired prime minister whose palatial property included private stables built for his family's use, as Libyan women were not permitted to ride in public.

As part of a group of officers, diplomats, and politicians, we were among five other couples invited to a formal dinner at the home of the former prime minister, and it was fabulous! The husbands were ambassadors from European and Middle Eastern countries; I was the only non-diplomat in the group. Enjoying a sumptuous meal, our dinner group discussed literature, art, and music. At one point I thought the group might be impressed to know I had played the saxophone in college. With my interjection, everyone stopped talking and looked at me as though I had just announced that I was from another planet. Apparently they did not consider the "sax" a musical instrument, but a bawdy-sounding invention of swamp-dwelling Americans. I guess I should have told them I played the cello. I didn't bring up my proud accomplishments again that night, but Genevieve held up the conversation for both of us, elegantly conversing in French, English, Arabic, and Italian. Her sophistication amazed me. Our social life really took off because of her, and we attended more cocktail and dinner parties.

On weekends and holidays our family took day trips to the great historic and cultural sights of Libya. Our social group organized a trip to an extinct volcano in a remote southern area. About thirty of us boarded an old DC-3 plane and flew to Sebha, near the Sudan border, to clear customs. At the airport a group of Libyan officials politely offered me some tea and refreshments. I thought it was peculiar to be treated as a VIP, but I soon found out that as I look Italian they had mistaken me for the Italian ambassador. I must admit that I enjoyed feeling important for a few minutes, but I never understood why we had to clear customs because we weren't leaving the country.

According to a geologist traveling with us, the volcano we had come to see had last exploded some 60,000 years ago. We reached our destination at sunset, a bit apprehensive as we landed on sand in the middle of the desert, but we made it. The sun went down in a riot of rich hues. We quickly put our tents up, ate a light dinner, and crawled into our sleeping bags just as the night chill fell. The next morning we arose to a spectacular sunrise and breathtaking view of the ancient volcano-within-a-volcano, surrounded by seven brackish lakes. What a sight to behold! The sand near the volcano was black on top and cream-colored just beneath. Walking on it our footsteps broke through the thin upper layer to expose the lighter layer. The geologist explained how the coarser black sand would shift back to the surface in a few days, and our white footprints in the black expanse would disappear. He cautioned us on the instability of the terrain, caused by wind and water erosion in deep gullies and dry ancient river beds. We hiked over the outer crater to descend into the shallower inner crater and then crossed to the other side, exiting there and circling back to where we had started.

We spent another night sleeping on the desert floor. The next morning as we were loading the plane we saw on the distant horizon four tiny dots moving towards us. In about forty minutes we realized a man and three women were walking across the desert. They were smiling and seemed happy. As they approached us, one of the professors in our group spoke with the man, who indicated that the women, who wore gold rings through the sides of their noses, were his wives. They needed medicine and water. We accommodated them the best we could, giving them what we had: a few aspirins and a jug of water. I took photos, and we all said goodbye. I don't know how they survived or navigated in the desert, as there was nothing around for hundreds of miles. They came from nowhere and went to nowhere.

Before boarding I noticed a good-sized rock near my foot and picked it up. It was shiny and looked like a piece of black glass. The professor said it was thousands of years old, formed when the volcano erupted. Not only did I have a memorable visit, I also had a gem of a souvenir. We all held our breath as the plane taxied over the black sand and soon lifted into the air. We had a last look of the ancient volcano before turning and heading north back to Sebha and then to Tripoli. I have some spectacular photos of this trip, particularly of the ancient volcano in the heart of the Sahara desert, and this adventure's rich images remain vivid in memory.

Tripoli enthralled us with its magnificent Mosques, lively Suks or street markets, and fascinating architecture. It had the biggest camel-trading market in the world, and noisy caravans filled its roadways.

The coastal drive west towards Tunisia featured mountain scenery and villages of white mud huts. On one trip we toured a huge cave where imprisoned British POWs, captured by the Germans during World War II, had painted a wall mural of the North African and Libyan coast, depicting its curving bays and peninsulas as the alluring figure of a nude woman.

On other trips we took in Libya's many ancient ruins, both Greek and Roman, still well preserved. Also to the west, we visited Sabratha, a Roman site, which included luxurious heated public baths and the opulent theater housing the stunning marble statues of the Three Graces. Heading east the incredible ruins of Leptis Magna captured our interest. The Romans were far ahead of their time, considering the general conditions of their era.

On one of our driving trips, we stopped out of curiosity to talk to some men we saw working not far off the winding road. We greeted each other, using the usual politely closed hands and slight bow of the head. We exchanged some words in Italian, and Genevieve was able to speak to them in Arabic. The men were uncovering an ancient mosaic floor, sweeping sand from it. When they asked if we wanted to help, we replied, "Yes, of course!" Sweeping the sand, we realized we were uncovering a Roman floor that hadn't been seen in over two thousand years. Our eyes feasted on the glorious colors and workmanship. The decorative tiles were beautifully preserved. I got goose bumps and still do to this day when I think about it. I was not permitted to take pictures because the "boss man" was not there. I offered a little bakshish (money) but they refused. They were so kind and friendly. We parted with clasped hands and thanked

Tuareg tribal dancers

them with their word "Choukran." This was another experience I never forgot.

We watched the men of Tuareg tribe in the Fezzan area in southern Libya perform traditional dances around a campfire. They cover their faces, except for a tiny slit for their eyes. Some distance away, more historic ruins are found in Cyrenaica. Originally built by the Greeks and then occupied by the Romans, it is known as the birthplace of Simon of Cyrene, who is said to have stepped in to help Jesus when he stumbled under the weight of the cross.

It is regrettable that the Libyan government and its people were not creating a tourist environment for people to come and enjoy these ancient civilizations. It would be good for our understanding and knowledge about what Libya can offer to the rest of the world in terms of history, culture, and architecture. When I look at my pictures of Libya I often wonder how these ruins look today and whether they will be preserved for future generations. At this writing, the future for viewing these sights is not very bright.

***

I maintained regular phone contact with my parents, who had retired from chilly New Jersey to balmy Florida ten years earlier. Dad now enjoyed his gardening hobby all year 'round in the mild weather. Growing and cultivating delicious fresh produce had always given him great satisfaction, and in Florida he found his paradise.

In the summer of '71 our family joined together in celebrating the joyful occasion of our parents' 50th wedding anniversary. It did my heart good to be with my family. During the following school year, my sister Jean called me to say Dad was in the hospital following a stroke, unable to speak and with his left side paralyzed. The doctors gave us some hope that therapy might help him regain his abilities. Two weeks later, however, Jean called again, with the sad and sudden news that Dad passed away. For us to lose him at the age of 76 was an unexpected tragedy.

He was a man from simple beginnings who had come to America for a new life, fought bravely as an American in the war, and built a good life for his family. He was a contributor to society, and a person who possessed extraordinary common sense. I took emergency leave and flew back to Florida for Dad's funeral, and stayed by Mom's side most of the time. She was strong and brave, dealing silently with her loss.

***

Back at Wheelus Air Base, I was involved with my work. Our base schools participated in exchange programs with Libyans, Italians, and British. Genevieve was occupied by her horses and riding lessons. Eric, too, rode horses, and he learned to scuba dive. He kept busy with studying and dating. Life was good. We were in good health and enjoyed spending time with dear friends.

In early August, 1969, a representative of an influential American business corporation dined at our home. We were discussing the stability of Libya. We felt that it was a sound country: the people seemed to be happy, prosperous, and enjoying life.

Yet, this businessman, and I'll never forget it, said, "No, don't you believe it. This country is ready for a coup, and it's going to be sooner than you think." This man was well traveled with many connections and had access to inside information. He either knew or sensed that something was about to happen and gave us fair warning. But I shrugged it off as casual dinner table conversation. A few weeks later, around August 30th, he tried to reach me and left a message. Over the next few days I was unable to reach him at his home or office. He had literally vanished, disappeared into thin air.

The start of the school year was about a week away, and I was getting ready. An item remaining on my to-do list was to have a number of broken musical instruments repaired. It was typical for these items to suffer wear and tear from student use, but I had been unable to find a repair shop in Libya, so I was working on arrangements to send them to Malta.

On a beautiful September Saturday before the semester began on Tuesday, I was at school. A worker at the facility told me the Arabs were not coming to work because something had happened to the king, that he was sick. It seemed a rather strange explanation, but, nonetheless, the janitors, carpenters, and other Libyans had not shown up. I was concerned that school would not be ready for opening day. About noontime, Genevieve, who had gone horseback riding, called and asked, "Have you heard? There are Libyan troops posted outside the base. The king is deposed, and there's been a coup." I was shocked. I couldn't believe it. She continued, "On my way to the stables, I saw Libyan troops lined up on both sides of the road, a short distance outside the base gate. I thought they were doing maneuvers of some sort, until I got to the riding club." There she was told that military rule had been imposed. Alarmed by the news and now frightened by the presence of troops, she immediately headed home. The soldiers allowed her to pass, and she arrived on base through the back gate. It was unlocked and no extra guards had been posted, as if it were any normal Saturday. Alarmed by this obvious security oversight, I phoned the information officer at base headquarters and related how my wife was able to leave base, drive through the countryside with Libyan troops everywhere, then come right back onto the base. While U.S. and Libyan forces cooperated to seal the main gate with tanks and armaments, blocking entry and exit, those in charge apparently had forgotten about the back gate. After my call, the major gave the order to correct the oversight.

King Idris was away in Egypt for medical reasons when Muammar Gaddafi, an ambitious colonel in the Libyan Air Force, organized the bloodless coup. He neutralized the civil police, and his officers completed the takeover in a few days without a shot being fired. Gaddafi was handsome and charismatic, and the Libyans seemed to accept his leadership. In the beginning he was not cruel. It was some time later that his political opponents had a tendency to disappear.

We listened to the base's radio station, but we could not obtain news of what was happening. Tuning to BBC radio, we learned that the Libyan radio station had been taken over, the airport closed, high-ranking Libyan officials taken into custody, including some of our business friends, and now Libya had a militant Muslim leader. We also heard all kinds of rumors involving firing squads and shootings, but none could be confirmed.

A week or so after the coup, an American Embassy official came to our home to speak with Genevieve about going into downtown Tripoli to make contact with certain individuals, gather information, and report back. It was assumed that with her French passport, Genevieve could proceed through the checkpoints without any difficulty. Fortunately or unfortunately, Genevieve's passport had expired, and she could not accommodate them. It seemed peculiar that the embassy official wanted to enlist a French national for this task.

About a week later we ventured downtown ourselves to visit friends and inquire as to their well-being. During the monarchy's ruling years there weren't any skirmishes over religious differences. Now, with a Muslim in charge of the country, we were particularly concerned about Alphonso, a Libyan Jew and owner of a very large and profitable Volkswagen dealership, whom Genevieve had befriended at the riding club. We spoke with an Italian doctor and his wife who related incidents of some local people breaking into the homes of Italians and Jews, roughing them up. They didn't know where Alphonso was and, like us, were worried about him.

The next day, Genevieve again met with the doctor at his request and learned that the couple was secretly providing refuge for Alphonso. Alphonso's wife and family had coincidentally left for Rome a few days before the coup, but Alphonso had stayed behind an extra day to go horseback riding, a decision that might just cost him his life. Hearing of door-to-door searches, the doctor was fearful of Alphonso being discovered and asked if we would take him into our home on the base until he could safely leave the country. When Genevieve related the request to me, I said, "Yes, by all means."

The following day, Genevieve met with Alphonso on one of the country roads near the riding club, as we had arranged. He left his car on the side of the road and jumped into the back seat of our car. Returning to the base with Genevieve, he broke down and wept with relief and gratitude as he entered our door.

Our home was comfortable but very small, only about 650 square feet. With two bedrooms, a living/dining room combination and a tiny kitchen, we had very little space for a fourth person. But we managed. We went about our usual routines and tried to live normally. We had to be careful, and we had to be quiet. Our walls were paper-thin, so we often heard our neighbors, and they heard us. Alphonso slept in the living room on a small army cot I had secured. We folded it up and put away in the daytime. When friends came over Alphonso hid in our walk-in closet! Several times we had dinner parties at our home. Since these lasted several hours, I took him to the school where he could rest more comfortably in the nurse's room. Late at night I went back to pick him up, as I feared that the Air Police would find him and turn him over to the Libyans if I left him there. We had some anxious moments hiding and ducking, careful not to arouse the suspicions of the guards.

This went on for several weeks. On base we heard many disturbing rumors of killings downtown and of the airport being closed. We felt left in the dark, unable to substantiate the hearsay or obtain the truth about what was happening. Base officials, if they knew, certainly were not saying anything.

Alphonso was terrified, and he knew he could not return home. Before he found refuge with the Italian doctor and his wife, a street mob had ransacked his apartment. They bashed his console stereo set into pieces, thinking it was some kind of a transmitter to send classified information, and reported him to military troops nearby. He was subsequently accosted by soldiers, labeled an Israeli spy, marched to the city square, and forced to stand with his hands in the air with four men pointing guns at him. An officer passing by recognized Alphonso and ordered his release, literally saving his life on the spot.

Alphonso wanted to contact his wife and children, as he knew they were concerned for his safety. This was not easy as international phone calls and outgoing mail were temporarily restricted in the aftermath of the military takeover. I found a roundabout way to contact Alphonso's wife, however, by using a new worldwide U.S. military telephone system known as Autovon.

I needed to call one of our teachers in Rome about his return flight schedule. After I spoke with him I remained on the line and asked the Autovon operator to connect me with another of our teachers in Rome. The call rang through, and amazingly, Alphonso's wife answered. I spoke cryptically: "Don't worry about the Italian teacher, he is safe and sound." I hoped she understood that Alphonso was with me, but I wasn't sure until years later when she expressed her gratitude and relief to get that message. She'd been holding to her belief that Alphonso was safe and would rejoin their family soon.

Alphonso began to feel walls were closing in on him and pressed me to get him out, one way or another. He was quite a businessman, and he had plenty of money, including a large sum of traveler's checks, lots of cash, and his checkbook. He was ready and willing to pay up to $20,000 for help. He suggested that I make some kind of an arrangement for him to fly. "Ask some of the pilots," he advised. "And tell them I'll be glad to pay them." Alphonso also proposed paying me a substantial amount for my assistance, but I vehemently refused his offer. If I were to help him, it would be because he was a fellow human being whose life was in danger.

I continued to consider ways to get him safely away, but I couldn't come up with a viable plan. I couldn't possibly get him on a military plane. I couldn't ask an American official to assist us. I didn't have confidence in the base officials to ask them for help, for I believed and feared they would simply turn him over to the Libyan authorities. But the longer he stayed with us, the more likely it was that he would be found out. Finally, a thought came to me: the musical instruments! That was the way! My plan, which I named "The Music Box," was high-risk, but there was a good chance it would work.

The musical instruments gave me a plausible reason to leave the country. Everyone knew that I had over fifty instruments that needed repair and that I was planning to send them to Malta for that purpose. Several of the boxes required to ship the assortment of mostly-brass instruments, including French horns, clarinets, trumpets, and awkwardly-sized tubas, would be fairly heavy, justifying the weight of an additional crate containing our friend. Still, there were many issues to be addressed. I needed orders for an air shipment, as well as approval to accompany the shipment. I required a large crate for Alphonso, but then how would he breathe? Would he get through customs? What if the crate he was in was treated roughly? Would he survive his ordeal? I had many decisions to make, and there wasn't much time.

I set my plan in motion by securing orders to ship the instruments and to attend a conference in Europe, via Malta. Beautiful! Perfect! Everything was falling into place. I began gathering and crating the instruments to be shipped. One shipping container from the school was large enough to add a false bottom under which Alphonso could hide. I equipped it with a breathing tube to use through a hole that popped open via a loose knothole, as well as a hammer and screwdriver. In the event of an emergency, he could pound his way out of the box. When we tested the space, Alphonso, a slim man of about 150 pounds, fit without a hair to spare. We were ready!

On the eve of our scheduled flight, Alphonso again offered me money for helping him escape. Again, I refused. I indicated, however, that a contribution of 140 Libyan pounds to cover the cost to repair the school's instruments would be accepted, and he immediately wrote a check to the school. That was all the money involved in this transaction.

The night before, I sat down with Genevieve and wrote out a letter, a statement to be given to the commander in the event something went terribly wrong. The letter stated as follows:

> *I am about to undertake something which to me may be the most important contribution I could make to my fellow-man. I realize the responsibilities and the consequences in the event I am caught. However, I am willing to risk all to help. For the first time in my life, I can see the results of hate, fear, and war. Now I know what it means to be fearful of one's life; to run and hide; to be concerned that one may not see their loved ones again. To be afraid to the point of taking your own life before being caught by a people whose only hatred of an individual is because he is a Jew and not because he has done something wrong. I cannot shirk my responsibility as a human, as an American, to help this individual. I realize, if caught, the embarrassment it may cause my country and family—but to me, the joy of helping someone is worth it. No*

one knew about this plan except my wife, not one military
man at Wheelus, nor my friends. I did not receive help; it
is my sole responsibility. Please let it be known that I would
have helped an Arab or anyone else under the circumstances.
I am not doing this for money, nor for personal glory, but for
the sake of a person whose only crime was being born a Jew.

I had no choice in this matter, and I was prepared for the consequences. Genevieve, sweet Genevieve, always loving, agreed that I needed to do this, and she was not going to stand in my way. We feared that if I turned my friend over to the military authorities, they would simply turn him over to the Embassy people, who would turn him over to the Libyans. How could we live with that?

Early the next morning before the neighbors were up, Alphonso and I crept quietly out of the house and went to the school. I helped him into the crate where he curled up tightly like a baby in the fetal position, and I wrapped a pillow around his head in case the box was jostled in transit. I enclosed the hammer, screwdriver, and air hose in his hiding place and made sure the knothole was loose, so he could punch it out if needed.

Minutes seemed like hours waiting for the airbase supply workers to pull up at the back of the school and load the carefully packed wooden crates and cardboard boxes onto the flatbed truck. School was just getting underway, and the children and teachers were arriving. I felt a sigh of relief as the driver and his assistant lifted Alphonso's crate onto the truck and did not consider it unusually heavy or large. I climbed into the truck with the men and rode along to the airport at Wheelus Air Force base. We drove directly onto the tarmac, pulling up next to the Air Force transport plane. The pilot said he might have to put all the instruments in the belly of the plane. This gave me some consternation because it might be too cold and lacking in oxygen, but then he suddenly changed his mind. "No, let's store them behind the passenger compartment," he decided. "It will be a lot easier and quicker to unload." This was much better, but the crate with Alphonso was placed on its side, not upright as we had planned, causing me concern regarding Alphonso's comfort and safety.

Genevieve had driven to the airport, so we could see each other one last time before I embarked on this dangerous journey. As I was about to board the flight, I tenderly kissed her, and then I walked to the plane, turned around, and waved. In my memory I can still see Genevieve in her elegant green suit waving back. I was somewhat worried, but I really believed that my wife and son would be flown out without any difficulty, if something went wrong on this venture. After all, I was the so-called culprit, the action man, and the American military would ensure the safety of my family.

It was a rough, bumpy flight through a storm. Circling over Malta the pilot informed us that if we couldn't land due to the rain and the high winds, we'd have to return to Libya. At this announcement I was overcome with fear, but I sat quietly and tried to retain my composure. The hours were slipping by. My friend had been cramped in the crate since 6 A.M., and we had loaded the plane at 8 A.M. Here it was close to noontime, and we didn't know when, or where, we would be landing. Suddenly this skilled military pilot proclaimed, "There's a clearing! We are going to try to make it. If not by this approach, we'll turn around and go back." I took a deep breath of renewed hope. After he landed the plane and we taxied to the terminal, I felt much better. Later I realized that this was only the first leg of a very complex adventure, one that changed the course of our lives.

SIX

Escaping Malta

After clearing customs at the Malta airport, I called a local trucking company to pick up the shipment. I had not been able to arrange a delivery truck from Libya, so this was short notice. None were available. After pleading and begging, I convinced them to send a truck with two helpers. As the truck approached, my heart sank. I had been hoping for a covered truck, where I could have extracted Alphonso without being seen, but it was an open flatbed. And there were other problems. When the flight's loadmaster, a large burly man, moved the box from its side, I was astonished to see perspiration dripping from it. In fact, the entire box was soaking wet on one side! The loadmaster, wearing heavy gloves, didn't notice.

My shipment also had to clear customs. Alphonso and I had developed a code, so I could determine if he was all right. When I tapped three times on the crate, he was to respond with three taps. If he didn't, I was to get a hammer and chisel and open the crate immediately. But he responded, and I was quite relieved. Customs opened one crate, looked at the instruments, and waved us through. Next stop: Nani's Music Shop in Valletta.

It was unbelievable how steep and narrow the streets were in that city. Riding in the cab of the truck I wondered if we would make it, but we did. Yet our travails were not over. At the store I was told that there was no room for the instruments, "You must take them to our warehouse, located across town." So back we went, literally driving across the city and into the countryside to a small village about twelve kilometers away. Then the warehouse turned us away, informing us that there was no room for

85

all of those musical instruments and telling us to take them back to the music shop! No amount of discussion changed the warehouse manager's mind. Not having any choice, we turned the truck around.

Heading back towards Valletta, we passed a Catholic church. I thought we could stop there and leave the boxes with the priest, as churches often help in situations such as this. But the truck was moving quickly, and I hesitated. We drove on. By now, I was desperate. Worried about Alphonso, I asked the driver to stop. He did. I asked him and his helper, "Would you mind if the two of you take a little break, and walk away some distance from the truck?" They were puzzled, but obliged me. As soon as they walked off, I went to the back of the truck, and with a hammer and screwdriver I had in my briefcase, opened the crate containing Alphonso. Literally, he came crawling out. After ten hours enclosed in the tight space, he could hardly move. Once he began stretching to get the circulation back into his arms and legs, he was in pretty good shape. What now, I thought. I asked if he wanted to jump off the truck and escape into the bushes, but no, he preferred to stay with the truck. I waved for the driver and his helper to come back, but apparently they had spotted Alphonso and both men took off running wildly down the road, abandoning their truck! I knew then and there we were in trouble.

I quickly told Alphonso that for his safety he should find his own way out of Malta. He stopped a passing car, hopped in, and took off. That was the last time I saw Alphonso.

My troubles were just beginning. I immediately went in the back of the truck to reseal the crate. As I jumped out, I was almost struck by a speeding car. It missed me by inches. I hailed another car going in the other direction and asked the driver to take me to the military airport.

At the airport I entered the terminal, trying to appear calm and composed, to be greeted with the news that my departure had been delayed an hour, as the pilot had not yet returned. I really needed to get out of there, and things were not going my way. Finally, as the passengers were lined up to board, a police inspector and some of his detectives arrived asking for the man who had ordered the truck for the musical instruments. To my chagrin, the truck driver had accompanied them and pointed me out.

The questioning began. They asked me about an extra man on the truck. "That's not possible," I said. Playing dumb, I told them I had left all the cargo on the truck, which the driver was to deliver to the music shop. So we went to the truck, now parked at the airport entrance. "Let's open the crate," the inspector directed. I wasn't concerned about the detectives finding incriminating evidence, as I had tossed the pillow and breathing tube into the bushes and gotten rid of the false bottom, when I had freed Alphonso. The opened crate revealed only musical instruments.

Still, the police inspector wasn't satisfied, and he asked me more questions. I held my ground, insisting that there was no other man. Back and forth we went on this issue. At one point, even the driver's assistant, who had been very quiet, began to wonder if the driver had imagined seeing the man. Finally, about seven in the evening, the inspector said we were all to go to the station. I wanted to know why. He explained that the matter was not resolved to his satisfaction, and by law, he was able to hold suspects for two days without giving them a reason.

At the station, I thought I could secure my release by telling the inspector that my flight was being held for me and I was expected back in Libya. After all, I had not been arrested. In fact, this word had never been mentioned. "No, we called the airport," he replied. "We are holding and detaining the airplane until we clear this matter." And he asked for my passport. I refused to hand it over, insisting, "I will not give my passport to anyone but an American Embassy official." This was perhaps the biggest mistake I made in this entire affair, but I was only doing what I thought was the right thing, to ask for representation from my embassy. I believed I would be protected, and I felt confident the embassy would sympathize with my situation. I was soon to learn, however, how the U.S. State Department works, how they "assist" their citizens abroad.

I refused to speak to a Maltese detective waiting with me in the interview room at the police station, telling him, "I will not discuss this matter in the presence of anyone from the police department." He eventually left. In the meantime the inspector, still leery regarding my denial about another man, ordered a search for any suspicious-looking person of small stature on the island. And it was a small island with many others fitting the same description.

Another three hours passed before two officials from the State Department and a Navy man in uniform arrived. When asked, I handed my passport to them and explained to the officials how I had brought out a Libyan Jew whose life was threatened following the military coup. This man was a friend, I told them, and I undertook this effort for humanitarian reasons, to save a life. Indeed, I told them everything. I also indicated that I was very worried about being questioned further by the Maltese government and made it clear that I had not disclosed my story to the police. "You can tell them anything," I exclaimed. "They don't know who I brought out! You can tell them I had a mistress!"

My countrymen were not receptive to my idea. The embassy man said sternly, "No way. We're going to be open, honest, and direct. We'll tell them everything you told us." And, in that moment, my hope dissolved. I realized I should not have asked for the embassy's help. These officials, who I had expected to apply wise discretion to my dilemma, appeared to be the very people who could be my undoing.

Nor were my countrymen on my side. The Navy man snapped at me, "How do we know you are telling the truth?" And, would you believe it, his next question was, "How do we know you're not a spy? I see in your passport that you've been to Egypt several times. Why?" "Why?" I echoed. "I like Egypt. It's my favorite country." What was going on here, I wondered. "Wait a minute here," I questioned in turn. "What does Egypt have to do with what I just did?" The man replied, "Your name is Daniel. You're Jewish yourself, aren't you?" Blinking in disbelief, I asserted, "No, no, I am not Jewish. I'm Italian, American Italian. My parents came from Italy." They asked how much money I received for doing this. "Nothing, not a penny," I replied firmly.

The questions, mostly ridiculous, kept coming. I decided that I'd be better off if I didn't answer. I thought these people were here to help Americans abroad. I thought their job was to offer advice and guidance with sympathy and understanding. Instead, they insensitively called me "dumb," "stupid," and "crazy" for what I had done. I knew that I was dumb and stupid, as I had been told in the fourth grade, but I was never called crazy.

Enough was enough. I refused to answer any more of their questions. "I want to speak to the Ambassador," I informed them. "I will not say another word until I see the Ambassador." I believed the Ambassador, given his intelligence and tact, would be able to handle such a delicate matter, rather than blowing the situation out of proportion. When one of the officials began dialing, he was muttering, "Yes, I have got to call the Ambassador! This is the biggest thing that has happened to me in my eighteen years of foreign service. I must call the Ambassador!" I could not believe what I was hearing. Reaching the Ambassador, the man gushed, "Mr. Ambassador, Mr. Ambassador, it's really big, Mr. Ambassador. It's really big. I can't say it over the phone, but we will need the code man and the code book. We will have to wire Washington. It's really big, Mr. Ambassador, it's really big."

Listening to one side of the conversation, I felt as though the floor were falling out from under me. This official was overreacting. It would have been so much better to stay calm. The Ambassador, attending a dinner engagement, refused my request for an immediate meeting, but indicated that he would come the next morning. I made it clear that I was through, absolutely through, talking to these embassy men. They left me at the station in care of the Maltese police, where I would remain until I appeared before a judge the next day.

I had never spent a night in jail, and my outlook was bleak. The police took away my shoelaces, belt, fountain pen, nail clipper, tie, and my jacket, for fear, I suppose, that I might hurt myself. They escorted me into a small room with only a cot and mattress. I must have been a model prisoner, however, as they left the door open all night!

I spent a restless night. The cell was dark and old. Cracks ran through the walls, and loose chunks of plaster appeared ready to drop. I tossed and turned, worried about how the embassy people were reacting. My future did not look very bright. I eventually realized I really should have told the police everything right from the start.

While still resting on my cot the next morning, I was startled when an employee trudged past my cell pushing a cart loaded with all the musical instruments and the large wooden crate, Alphonso's crate from which I had helped him escape... I hoped! The whole lot had been confiscated as evidence, and not knowing what to do with it, apparently they moved it to the police station. As the cart seemed to pass by in a slow-motion eternity, all the recent crazy events raced through my mind, and I thought of my dear Genevieve and son Eric. What they must be going through right now! Yet I did not fear for them because I believed the base would immediately fly them out, as I knew they had done in previous situations involving military personnel or civilians. I recognized that this situation would be rather disruptive for Genevieve and Eric, but the man who faced the greatest consequences had escaped, to my great relief.

I was fully awake by the time the police returned my personal effects and brought me a breakfast tray! What a difference from the day before: these officers were kind and treated me very well. After I had eaten I was taken to a room equipped with fifteen to twenty telephones to be interviewed by a stout, burly police inspector. Despite his appearance, he had a friendly demeanor, but he was also very clever, trying to stir my emotions. He told me that the American Embassy official had told him about my Jewish friend, and he was concerned, suggesting, "Maybe we can help him if he is hurt or something happened to him." He tried to convince me that the best thing to do was to give a description of the man so they could find him, but I refused to reveal any details. Then the inspector turned to another line of questioning: "How did you know this man? Where did you find him? Where did you meet him? Who are his friends in Libya?" Again I did not give him any information. When he asked how much money this man had given me, I answered truthfully, as I had previously: "There was not a penny involved."

Our discussion went on for perhaps several hours. At one point the inspector said sincerely, "I believe you. I really want to help him." He confided, "You know, I really don't like the Libyans myself. They come to Malta for women and liquor, which they can't have in their own country. They're abrasive and abusive, and I really don't like them, these Libyans. Now let me help this man for you. Please tell me what he looks like." I simply couldn't trust this man. I wanted to, and I should have, but, unfortunately, I couldn't. In retrospect I should have cooperated more fully, but after my experience with the American officials on the previous day, I felt I couldn't trust anyone! Later on, I found out what a good man this police inspector was.

The rest of the morning one guard watched over me. He had a newspaper, but he wouldn't let me see it, so I didn't learn if my fiasco had made the news. We only exchanged a few words in English about the weather and Malta.

My next visitor was from the U.S. Embassy. He introduced himself as Mr. Green. "I'm here to help you," he said kindly. "What may I do for you?" I replied, "Yes, thank you! I'd like to buy some supplies, so I can clean up." He accommodated my request, returning with some shaving items, soap, and a towel. I washed and was ready to meet the ambassador.

The Ambassador, a tall, distinguished man, arrived about noon. He queried, "Say, what about this political leader that you brought out? Who is he? What do you know about him?"

It seemed that I was back to step one, and we repeated my conversation of the day before with the American officials. Yes, I had brought out a Libyan Jew. No, no money was exchanged, as this was a humanitarian effort. Yes, I proposed putting forth a story to save us embarrassment. "No," the Ambassador replied. "We're going to be truthful and to tell everything. We are not going to cover up for anything or anybody." Instead, he had come to an arrangement with the Maltese officials. I was to go to court and plead guilty. After I paid a fine of a hundred pounds, the equivalent of $280.00, the Maltese authorities would grant my release from their jurisdiction.

The Ambassador added, "Upon your release, you will go to a hotel and stay there. The next morning you will report to my office, where we have worked out a contingency plan with Washington. These are your instructions."

I thanked the Ambassador for his assistance and proceeded to court, escorted by the police inspector with whom I had been dealing. Waiting for my case to be heard was not easy, as the inspector planted doubts in my mind, despite the Ambassador's assurances. He thought the court would release me, but maybe not. He commented that the judge might be in a bad mood because it was late afternoon. He noted that we had disrupted the judge's routine, as we had asked him to return to court after leaving for the day. I was on edge, and began to wonder if I would get a jail term. I worried about my family, and that was most troubling of all.

***

Finally, I was to learn my fate. Upon entering the courtroom, I noticed the Embassy officials already seated at a table facing the judge's seat, as well as Mr. Green, who had thoughtfully brought me shaving equipment. I nodded a greeting to him. As I took my seat, he leaned over and said, "Excuse me, but what about paying me for that shaving equipment... the cream and soap I brought to you this morning?" Embarrassed at my careless oversight, I said, "Oh yes, certainly!" It had completely slipped my mind. I must have been too worried to think straight.

"How much do I owe you?" "About a dollar and forty cents," he whispered. I pulled some American and Maltese coins out of my pocket and held them out, so together we began picking out the exact change. Just then the judge called the court to order and the inspector tugged my other arm and said, "Stand, stand." We got up so quickly that I still had my hand open with the change. As we stood facing the judge counting the coins together, the clerk began reading the charges against me. It must have looked most peculiar. Apparently this official thought he'd better get his money back before I was thrown in jail.

The charge was aiding and abetting an alien to enter the shores of Malta without proper papers. The judge sternly demanded, "What do you plead in this matter, sir?" "Guilty, your honor," I replied. He smacked down the gavel and announced, "A fine of one hundred pounds. Please pay the clerk." It was all over in a matter of minutes, or so it appeared.

As with everything else in this fiasco, there was a problem. The Ambassador and I had not discussed the form in which my fine would be paid. The court, of course, would not accept a check in American dollars, and I only had thirty-some dollars in my pocket, as well as an American Express card. When I made known my dilemma, the judge, in frustration, exclaimed, "Everything was supposed to be arranged! Why don't you have the money?" My anxiety was rising again, and I replied to the judge, "Frankly, sir, I do not carry hundreds of dollars around in my pocket."

Since I couldn't be released until the fine was paid, the inspector suggested that I borrow the money from the embassy. One of the American officials called the embassy to see if I could write a check that the embassy would cash. I held my breath until he returned to say, "Yes, it can be arranged, but it will take about an hour for the treasurer to go to the embassy to open the safe and pick up the money." With a big sigh of relief, I quickly wrote the check and handed it to him before anyone changed their mind. At this point the official looked at it and asked doubtfully, "How do I know there are sufficient funds in the bank to cover this check?" I couldn't believe it! What was it with these guys? Why did they have to complicate things? I told him my recent earnings had been deposited and the check would clear. I also offered my American Express card as an option. Finally, he accepted my explanation and left.

The judge continued to fume, and I continued to worry. But an hour later, the American official came back with the hundred pounds. The judge reconvened the court and again stated, "One hundred pounds. Please pay the clerk." I walked over to the clerk and handed him the money. With a sigh of exasperation the judge announced, "Case dismissed!"

A police detective, who worked for the inspector, took me to a hotel near the shore to stay that evening. He considerately asked if I had money to pay the hotel bill, which I did. Before leaving he reminded me that I was to report to the American Embassy in the morning, as if I could forget. After a good meal, I wrote to Genevieve to explain everything that had transpired.

Early the next morning, I went to the airport to ask the pilot flying to Libya to deliver my letter to Genevieve. He told me that the embassy officials had instructed him to wait for me. Well, that didn't feel right. I told him, "No way am I going back to Libya!" and I left. I proceeded to the embassy as instructed, but I had a queasy hunch I was doing the wrong thing. I began thinking I should get out of Malta on my own, rather than awaiting orders from Washington.

In the embassy lobby I ran into Mr. Green, and we had a nice chat. I expressed concerns about returning to Libya, assuming that was my fate, when he suggested, "You know that we can't hold you here. You are free man. You're not being held under arrest and are free to go." I protested, but he repeated himself. "All I am saying is that you are not under arrest and are free to go." Although anxious about the situation, I had enough of my wits about me to realize he made a good point: get out of there while the getting was good. And I decided to do just that.

Trying to look as relaxed as possible, I headed for the door. "Where are you going?" an embassy official asked. "For a walk," I replied casually. "I need some fresh air." He let me pass, but his last words haunted me as I exited the building: "Don't forget now, come back in a few minutes. We've wired Washington to tell us what to do." Strolling down the street and looking in store windows, I took my time. I had a strange feeling someone was watching me. When I turned the corner, lo and behold, there was a taxi cab, and I jumped in.

Returning to the airport, I noticed a considerable number of people lined up at the Alitalia counter for a flight to Rome and learned the flight was sold out. Now what, I wondered, when someone tapped me on the shoulder. My heart froze, and I turned: it was an airport policeman. He said, "Come with me, please." I was in a panic, thinking the embassy knows I'm here, but I followed him to a back room where my friend, the inspector, sat at a table. Once more he had come to my rescue with invaluable assistance. "Do not go south," he advised. "Whatever you do, do not go south." For emphasis, he added, "Do not go back. I caution you. Do not go back." I had come to the same conclusion myself, but I explained that the flight was full. The inspector fixed that problem at the ticket counter, ordering the clerk to get me on the plane. With a small salute, the clerk wrote out the ticket and told me, "That will be a hundred and two dollars." Luckily I had my American Express card.

I thanked the inspector profusely, but he was not done. He showed me to a large room where he told me to wait until the plane left in an hour. With a sigh of relief, I felt this ordeal would soon be over. About forty minutes later the inspector returned. "Sorry, we're going to have to move you," he told me. "The plane is delayed, and it's risky for you to stay at the airport, so we want you to come with us." Once again, I followed him down a stairwell and out a side door. Believe me, I never realized there were so many entrances and exits to an airport terminal. Outside, he instructed, "You go with this man, and he'll get you back here in time, if the plane will be leaving. We're not sure now if the plane can take off due to the storm and high winds. In fact, call me in several hours, and I'll let you know exactly when to return." I got into the car, and we drove off.

My driver took me to a rather large and pleasant old hotel and indicated that I was to have lunch and call the inspector at two o'clock to see if the plane was scheduled to depart. After lunch, I had a couple of hours, so I bought some postcards to send to family members. The only thing I told them was that I was "visiting Malta." I also wrote to Harold Corbin, the famous lawyer who had defended the U.S. Cabinet members implicated in the Teapot Dome oil lease scandal of the early 1920s and a friend of Genevieve's. I wrote another postcard to Dr. Mason, Director of Dependent Schools, and told him that I had some difficulties, but I was hoping to be in Germany shortly. The next card I wrote was to my brother-in-law, a lieutenant colonel with the U.S. Army in Germany, saying I hoped to contact him shortly. Bill, an American, was married to my wife's sister Suzanne. Like Genevieve, she had studied English and was fluent in several languages. At two o'clock I called the inspector. He gave me the good news that a car was waiting in front of the hotel to take me to the airport, as my plane was leaving in forty minutes. There was no time to lose.

I walked outside the hotel apprehensively—all this cloak and dagger business! A man immediately approached to drive me to the airport. We entered through the same side door, and the inspector, waiting for me, sent me directly to the boarding area. I again thanked him with the utmost sincerity for his help, and I apologized for causing him some problems. He shrugged off my comments, telling me, "Take care of yourself. Just remember, don't go south." Those were his last words as he turned away. I wondered why he repeated them. I knew I was absolutely not going back to Libya.

Waiting to depart, who should appear but the two American embassy officials whom I had first met several days ago at the police station. They might have been doing their job, but I considered them pesky. Once more they questioned me: "Where are you going? What are you doing? Why aren't you staying here? Why aren't you going back to Libya?" I was not going to talk to them, and I told them so. "I thought I could trust you, and look what has happened! The Maltese are the ones who have really helped me—not my American brethren. Not the State Department, and not the American Embassy."

They continued to press me. "No, no, no, we want you to remain here for processing to return to Libya. Washington cleared the way for you to go back." "What guarantees would I have if I go back?" I asked skeptically. Of course, there were no guarantees, so I tried to conclude the conversation. "No, gentlemen, sorry, but I'm going north, not south," I said.

Even as I readied to board, they hounded me, begging and pleading for me to stay. One of the men, the one who cashed my check at the embassy so I could pay my court fine, to my utter disbelief, said, "Look, are you sure you have sufficient funds to cover that check?" I couldn't believe this man's suspicious nature! I assured him that I did. I added, "You can always garnish my salary. After all, I'm a federal government employee! Don't worry, the American government will get their two hundred and eighty dollars back." With that, I walked up the steps to the plane and bid my farewell. "Goodbye gentlemen, I'm going to Rome."

On the plane a burly, tough-looking man needing a shave sat in the seat across from me. He didn't say anything, but I could tell he was sizing me up with his half-closed eyes. "Oh, no, what am I getting myself into? Is he a friend or foe?" I asked myself. "Is he a policeman or someone who wants to take me into custody?" Boy, was I paranoid. I waited nervously for takeoff. Finally, the plane taxied down the runway, but then it turned back and taxied down the runway again. "Sorry folks, but we may not be able to take off due to inclement weather," the pilot announced. "We have some pretty strong headwinds and crosswinds, and

I'm afraid that we may not be able to make it. We'll just idle here until we see an opening in the clouds."

I was beginning to doubt I would ever get off the island.

SEVEN

Hostage Crisis

A break in the clouds was exactly what the pilot was looking for. "Folks, we're going to try it," the pilot broadcast. "I believe we'll be able to make it without any difficulty and I can assure you that it's not dangerous, although it might be rather bumpy." I leaned back and closed my eyes, saying a little prayer as the plane lifted off the runway and into the churning, angry sky. We were on our way to Rome!

Upon landing, I bought a ticket to Frankfurt on my American Express card, which literally was a lifesaver through this whole ordeal. I looked around at the crowd and to my relief, I didn't see the burly-looking character who'd been seated across from me on the flight from Malta. While I was waiting for the flight, I tried to figure out a way to contact Alphonso's family in Rome. I hadn't brought the phone number with me, so I looked in the phone book and there must have been a thousand of the same surnames in the book. It seemed impossible, so I sadly gave up.

I chose Germany as my next destination because I had in-laws there. Genevieve's sister and her husband Bill Mullins, a colonel, lived in Mannheim. Bill, originally from Tennessee, was an exceptional person with many contacts. I thought if anyone could help me sort through my problems and help me reach Genevieve and Eric, it was Bill.

First, I needed German marks. At the Frankfort airport, I tried to cash in my few remaining Libyan pounds. The window clerk refused the Libyan money. "Sorry, but with the problems in Libya, these pounds are no good."

I headed for another exchange window in the airport lobby. When I put down two Libyan pounds, this clerk also shook his head. Desperate for cash, I exchanged a few of my last U.S. dollars for some marks. In the meantime, three big Germans were observing me carefully, and a fourth, a tough-looking man, was on my tail when I went to call Bill to tell him I was in the country on my way to visit him and Suzanne. He followed me to the station where I caught the train to Mannheim. I didn't see any of these men on my train, so maybe my situation was improving or, perhaps, they decided that this fumbling school employee with only some pocket change didn't fit the profile of an international spy.

Once in Mannheim I related the entire story to Bill, who offered to check with his connections in Washington to help with this problem. The next morning I traveled to Karlsruhe to report to Dr. Mason, the DoDDS director for the region and an old friend who might be able to offer some good advice. Although the American military personnel in Germany had briefed him on my situation, he was unfamiliar with the details, and I emotionally filled him in. He was very sympathetic and understanding, although he asked me, "Dan, did you do it for money? I want the truth." When coming from Dr. Mason, the repetitive question was not annoying, as it had been in Malta. As I had done in the past, I answered truthfully, telling him, "No, I did not do it for money. I did it because a man's life was in danger." To my great relief, Dr. Mason reassured me. "Dan, I believe you, and I will help you."

That meant so much to me, and Dr. Mason stuck by me as the situation continued to unfold. He offered to let me stay in his home for a few days until I got settled, and he let me know that he would keep me posted on events. I desperately wanted to call Genevieve in Libya, but he said, "No, Wheelus command will not allow any contact with your wife." "Well, surely they will fly her out if I can't go back," I said tentatively. He added, "Yes, so I assume. Don't worry, she'll be all right."

This conversation only elevated my anxiety. All along I believed that she and Eric would be flown out of Libya immediately, but clearly this had not happened. It had been six days since the Malta incident, and it felt like the longest six days of my life. I waited another day at his home, hoping for news of my family's release, but Dr. Mason wisely advised it would be best for me to "lay low for a while," as any exposure could have negative consequences. He suggested I stay with Bill and Suzanne, and he put my job status on "annual leave," preserving my seniority and GS level. I am forever grateful to Dr. Mason for recognizing how precious my fulfilling career with DoDDS was to me.

I was very concerned about Genevieve. I wanted to learn how she and Eric were faring and to tell her I was safe in Germany. Bill shared my concern and continued making phone calls. He went to the Consulate General's office in Stuttgart and then met with a personal friend of his, the commanding general in Heidelberg. What he learned was not good. There were no plans to release Genevieve and Eric, as we had feared.

It became clear that my family was being held on the airbase until I turned myself over to the authorities in Libya. In effect, they were being held hostage by the American military!

Upon hearing this news I collapsed and fainted, passed out cold in a state of shock. Bill and Suzanne shook me and patted my face, asking if I was okay. Their first thought was that I'd had a heart attack, but I regained consciousness. Once composed, but still anxious, I asserted that I wanted to take action against this terrible wrongdoing. Bill said, "Cool it, cool it. I'll look into it. You're in no condition to make these inquiries. I'll make another trip to Stuttgart, and I'll also call Genevieve to see what's happening." When he reached Genevieve, she confirmed that she was to remain at the base until I returned. But least she was all right.

While this was going on, a new Wheelus base commander, a very ambitious man, was brought in, as the commander I had worked under was retiring. This new man did not know me or my family. His priorities were for himself, his next promotion, and returning to Washington as a celebrated general. His inability to secure my return, which forced him to break his promise to the Libyans, embarrassed him.

I believe an agreement was made between Washington and the airbase command to hold my family indefinitely. The new commander then deceptively asserted that it was the Libyan government that would not release my wife and son until I came back.

I determinedly set to work reaching out to my friends and contacts for their assistance. I wrote home to my parents, brothers, sisters, and in-laws. We called Mr. Corbin, the New York lawyer, asking for his help and advice. Bill contacted Tennessee Senator Howard Baker, an old friend from his home state, and he agreed to assist us in our efforts.

Some of these efforts paid off; others didn't. I contacted several of my professor friends who had acquaintances in New York's political circles. They did what they could. My mother wrote to President Nixon on my behalf. His Undersecretary of African Affairs, Ambassador Newsom, had known Genevieve and me when his children attended our school in Libya. Newsom, answering on behalf of the President, replied, "Unfortunately, our hands are tied. At this time we can not assist in this matter."

I worried constantly, but kept busy with letters and calls. Meanwhile, I couldn't write to Genevieve, and she couldn't write to me. Finally, about four weeks later, I received a letter from her. A friend of ours had literally smuggled the letter out of the country! He was with the banking system and was returning to Germany after attending a meeting in Libya. We met so he could pass on her letter. I was elated, but its contents were disturbing. It occurred to me there might be things she couldn't put on paper.

Although Genevieve related that she was well and Eric was doing fine in school, she feared what the future might hold, as no resolution was in sight. She was glad I was safe in Germany, and then added, "We are going to lose everything, Dan." With those words from her, my heart fell.

With no other options I stayed with Bill and Suzanne's family in Mannheim. Bill continued his efforts on our behalf, making contact with military leaders, U.S. State Department officials, and base commanders. After several calls to Wheelus, he spoke to a colonel who informed him that Genevieve and Eric would not be turned over to the Libyans. "For their own safety," however, they were not permitted to leave the base. This was another disappointing blow. Restless for positive action, I continued to seek out many of my stateside friends, who in turn wrote to Senator Javits, Representative Wolfe, President Nixon, Senator Young, the American Jewish Congress, Secretary Rogers, Representative Watson, Senator Thurman, Ambassador Goldberg, and many others. Almost everyone acknowledged that an American citizen was being unfairly held and agreed that the situation was deplorable, but the state of affairs did not change.

Another ominous incident occurred. I put through a call to Genevieve and quite surprisingly, I reached her. I told her of my efforts to get her and Eric released, but mid-conversation we were disconnected. The next day a Mr. Russell, who was representing the U.S. Embassy and its ambassador in Libya, called to tell me that he was aware of the call I'd made to my wife. He further related that the ambassador was especially concerned that I "tell the truth, the whole truth, and nothing but the truth." I told him that I had told the truth in Malta, but no one believed me. They thought I was an international spy with connections to the Israelis and the Jewish community. "If they didn't believe me before," I asked him, "how do I know they're going to believe me now?" Ignoring my question, he further warned me that the ambassador might have to turn my wife and son over for interrogation if I didn't cooperate. Another threat involving Genevieve! Who was demanding her detainment, the Americans or the Libyans? I maintain that perhaps the Libyan government had not requested my wife and son's detention after all, but the American government and some of its military influences had orchestrated this hostage situation out of fear that my actions might cause a political crisis between the two governments during the Libyan overthrow.

Several days following this incident, a headline in the Herald Tribune grabbed my attention. It read: "Second Libyan Smuggled Out Aboard U.S. Air Force Plane." The article briefly reported how a Libyan liaison to the deposed king was put on an Air Force plane and smuggled to Germany with the aid of two colonels. The article hit close to home. I knew both colonels quite well: one was the recently retired base commander and the other still lived on base. In the second half of the article, to my shock and dismay, I was mentioned by name and my smuggling of a Libyan Jew in a box of musical instruments was revealed. My ire was further piqued by the statement that "Libya has asked for Mr. De-Carlo's return." I believe the U.S. faction was responsible for this falsehood because Libya had not nor had ever communicated with me verbally or on paper acknowledging the incident or asking me to do anything! There are other interesting facts about this case, as well as several other inaccuracies in the story, that I point out here.

The Libyan liaison's exit, although called the "second" smuggling, took place immediately following the coup, preceding my Malta incident by at least a week. However, the authorities didn't learn about it until nearly a month after I had fled to Germany.

The king's liaison, also referred to as a "bag man" or a "fixer," was wealthy and influential. His function was to maintain good relations between the king's cabinet and the U.S. military presence in Libya. I never found out whether the colonels had done it as a favor for a man they believed to be in danger or they had received financial compensation for their act, although I suspect the latter.

The bag man was taken to an American hotel in Wiesbaden. A base finance officer confided to me some time later that the liaison was still on the American payroll while in Wiesbaden, receiving paychecks regularly from the Wheelus Finance Office!

I believe that when the flight crew was interviewed about my case, the sergeant and loadmaster of my flight to Malta said that it wasn't the first time this had happened. The sergeant eventually reported these two colonels, and it made the papers. However, the State Department refused to discuss this first incident, citing its sensitive nature.

I learned later that the colonel still living on base and his family were moved out immediately following the incident. They were in the midst of dinner when they were told by base officials to grab their coats and rush to an Air Force plane for relocation. It also came to my attention that both colonels were given an Article Fifteen, that is, they were verbally disciplined. And that was that. The military protects their own, especially officers. As a civilian I had no such immunity, so my name and an incriminating summary of the Malta incident were written up for the whole world to read.

Although I didn't have all the facts from reading the news story, I was able to surmise many of the details and called Dr. Mason in an emotionally agitated state. "Did you read the paper today, sir?" He had not. I quickly related the gist of the article, exclaiming, "They're holding my family hostage, but the two colonels received only a slap on the wrist!" I asked for a meeting and headed for his office, newspaper in hand.

Dr. Mason, as Director of Dependent Schools, was a GS-18, the equivalent of a general. He was very understanding, but there was nothing he could do to bring my family out of Libya. He did everything in his power to help me, however. He ensured my safety, and he was able to get me on temporary duty assignment, or TDY, to collect a living wage. I was given part-time work in his office, allowing me some free time to devote towards securing the release of my family.

Some time around late October, Bill received orders from JAG, or Judge Advocate General, the army's legal division, to go to Washington. He was following up on his connections there to see what could be done about releasing Genevieve and Eric. Bill took along my notes and a number of drawings I had made of the incident. He met with military leaders and again reached out to Senator Baker, his old friend from Tennessee.

My hopes were high as I paced away the waking hours for the next few days, waiting for his progress report. Bill finally called late at night, but with bad news. "There's nothing you can do. You've got to go back if you want Genevieve and Eric out." I couldn't understand it! Had he sold me out? Somehow or other, the JAG general ordered him to tell me what to do. The idea was for me to be exchanged for Genevieve and Eric at the Tunisian border. They would exit while I crossed back into Libya. I was appalled and disillusioned. The Libyans had not requested my return. They had not sent me a document saying that they were holding my wife. So, with no official papers, I was told that Genevieve would not be released until I returned. I laid awake all night, thinking and worrying.

I couldn't handle these feelings of helplessness any longer! I wanted to know what was really happening and to plead my own case in person. Before dawn the next day I threw a few things in a small suitcase and left a note for Suzanne to apologize for leaving suddenly—and again relied on my American Express card, as I didn't have a penny, to purchase a ticket from Frankfurt to New York.

Upon arriving in the U.S., I called my brother-in-law, and he was furious. He said he had secured my job but I had to go back to Germany. He then emphasized the State Department's instructions that I must not make any contact with reporters, as they would try to break the story. I acknowledged these instructions but still followed through with my insistence on meeting with some of the officials who wanted me returned to Libya. Bill agreed to set up a meeting in Senator Baker's office the next day.

On the flight from New York to Washington D.C., I was seated next to an educated-looking woman a few years younger. Exchanging formalities, I learned she was a lawyer returning to D.C. and she happened to be Jewish, too. Pure luck! Her name was Marsha Swiss. After relating my hair-raising adventures, I asked if she would represent me in Senator Baker's office. She was quite interested in my story and agreed to meet me at Senator Baker's office the next day.

The senator's office was absolutely beautiful. It was plush and tastefully appointed. A number of State Department officials and Senator Baker's aides, about seven or eight all together, attended the meeting. Bill was not too happy that I brought a lawyer with me, but I was glad that I had. Bill was family, and in matters such as this, it was best to be represented by an outsider, or someone who was not emotionally involved in the case.

In so many words, the attendees conveyed that their hands were tied. They insisted that I must return to Libya in exchange for my wife and son. My lawyer asked for official documentation to this effect, but none was produced for security reasons. Nor were we permitted to see a telegram from base officials stating that I must return to Libya. Even Bill insisted that I should go back, stating, as he had before, that it was best for my family.

When I look back on the meeting, I believe that the Pentagon had given Bill a choice: It's either your career or your brother-in-law's. I understand Bill needed to preserve his position and protect his livelihood for the sake of his family, so he opted to follow orders. He didn't really have an option. In fact, Miss Swiss confidentially advised me, "If I were you, I'd limit my contact with the colonel."

But I didn't have to go along with the program. My argument was as follows: Genevieve was on an American installation in her American home. I was not ordered by the Libyan government to do anything, nor did they threaten me. I had not been shown any documentation that my wife and son would be released upon my return. There was not one word, written or verbal, from the Libyan government. Furthermore, it was common knowledge that the Libyans didn't check on flights going in or out of the base, and the U.S. military could have flown out Genevieve and Eric any time, to anywhere!

***

Needless to say, nothing was resolved in Senator Baker's office that day. Afterwards at the hotel, I called Ambassador Newsom, my acquaintance who had been the ambassador to Libya and now occupied a high-ranking position in the State Department. When we connected, he told me that he was sorry that there wasn't anything he could do to secure Genevieve's release, as it was contingent upon my return.

My sister Jean's husband Denny, in New Jersey, stepped in to help as well. Denny scheduled one more meeting that might produce results. He had set up an appointment with a Mr. Wilson, a former Defense Department official, and together we went to New York to see him. He listened attentively to my story and agreed to help. "It was a humanitarian act," he noted, "and we need more of these good deeds in the world to help humanity and mankind." He indicated that he was going to Washington to meet with President Nixon later in the month and he was prepared to bring the issue up with the president. He also advised me to "cool it," not going to the papers with my story until he heard from the president. I was encouraged that such a high-ranking official would speak with the President on my behalf. This, too, led to a dead end, as his meeting with the President was eventually cancelled.

I returned to Germany and waited. It was so difficult. The days were long, and I suffered even longer sleepless nights. My thoughts were always full of Genevieve and Eric. Would I ever see them again? What was their state of mind? How was their health? I wanted to call Genevieve, but I was still forbidden any contact. These orders came from my superiors, who, I believe, received these orders from even higher officials.

Bill received permission to visit my family in Libya, and he secretly took a letter I had written Genevieve in which I explained my thoughts, concerns, and fears. I detailed the hurdles I had faced and asked her forgiveness for the heartaches I had caused. I knew this wasn't pleasant for her, and that she was suffering and worried. We both knew I shouldn't return unless she was jailed or threatened. Our separation was agonizing, but I held firmly to the belief that it would not last forever, and I would never give up trying.

Bill returned home to Germany a week later and briefed me on a meeting he'd had with the base commander. He didn't disclose any details of the conversation, only saying, "I'm sorry, but no luck. Genevieve cannot come out unless you return."

My options were falling away one by one.

To keep up my spirits, I played again and again a cassette tape that Genevieve had sent back with Bill. She and Eric taped an "audio letter" for me.

"Hello, Dad. It's great to have a chance to talk to you now. Uncle Bill decided to take this tape to you. Well, since you've been gone, I've been staying on base and had to stop horseback riding and everything. I don't go off base because of the situation. I had to stop soccer also, because this year the games are going to be off base. But I went out for basketball, and we've been having practice for the past two or three weeks now. Tomorrow I'll know whether I made the team or not. I've done pretty good on my grades these nine weeks. I came up with four B's and two A's and, well, that's about all the news around here. I hope you are all right and well. Hope to see you soon. Love, Eric."

In spite of hearing of Eric's continued restriction to the base, it was comforting to hear his voice again! And then I heard Genevieve's lightly-accented voice, which had captivated my heart ten years before. It had me in tears.

"It's good to have a chance to make a tape for you, Dan, even though it is a one way conversation. We told you what we have been doing in our previous letter. Eric has been a good boy, although it has been hard for him to study. We wanted to find out more about the situation and any progress you might be making from Germany. It was nice to have Bill visit, but I am concerned about Eric and his safety. I am really afraid for him. Dan, I cannot tell you what the situation is like. We never leave the house without the Security Police following. I have a guard at night.

"Dan, it's not that I don't want to hear your voice or read your words, but I ask you not to write often, and especially not to telephone. Our best hope is to be as quiet as possible. The base is surrounded with armed Libyans. The colonel said today that the guards on the base will protect me. Well, I will hold on and keep my courage up. In case of a showdown, I still have that Spanish sword! I am working hard not to break down, and you must not break down either. I love you, you know, and ask you that we are in such a situation that you and I both must keep up our health and to think of our love for each other. I will try to write to you when I can, but without much detail, as the situation is being so confused here that… anyway, I cannot say much. I would also like you to set aside money because we have to start again from nothing. Well, Dan, try to have a lot of courage and also don't tell everybody about our problems as it might not be beneficial. You should not stay any longer with Dr. Mason's family. You just cannot have everyone share our troubles. Please don't try to send me anything unless it's necessary, and please do not try to call at all. It can only hurt us. I guess that's about all, my love. Believe me, I am anxious to see the end of this nightmare, and I hope to see you soon. I love you very much, and I miss you. Bye-bye."

These were the saddest words I had ever heard from her. The sound of her voice did my heart so much good, yet her fear and hurt were clearly apparent and shook me deeply. It was the longest communication we'd had since I left Libya two months before.

***

Another month passed. I was under extreme stress and becoming a nervous wreck. I went to the doctor for sleeping pills, and believe it or not, even they didn't help. He gave me just a few at a time, for fear I would take too many.

On a Friday around the fifth of December, I told Bill that I'd had it, that I wasn't going to wait any longer. And I gave him an ultimatum: if Genevieve and Eric were not freed by December 19th, our wedding anniversary, I planned to return to the States and give my story to the major news services. I deduced that having some snoopy newspaper reporters digging up dirt on this whole charade might shed light on the military's shenanigans and bring about some action. Something had to happen! Three months was a long time for my family to be held hostage. Bill was very upset with this, telling me I was being foolish, that I should think of my wife and my son. But my bluff worked. My message definitely got through to the "powers that be" because I received a call from Dr. Mason's wife Sue around December 10th. She called to ask, "Dan, are you going to be around this weekend?" Baffled by the question, I said, "Yes, certainly. Where else am I going to go?" She said, "Oh, I just wanted to know if you were going to be around. I thought I'd see how you were doing and all." I thanked her and thought she was kind to show concern.

That Sunday Sue called again asking the same questions. On Monday morning Dr. Mason's office called to say that Genevieve and Eric had just arrived in Italy! I later found out that over the weekend the Wheelus officials had tersely told Genevieve, "Pack your bags. You're leaving tomorrow morning." To her amazement and mine, they finally flew her and Eric to Aviano airbase in Italy, around the time Sue had called on Sunday afternoon.

On December 15th, Genevieve called me from Italy. She was drained from the ordeal but relieved to be back in Europe. She had only been allowed to take a few suitcases with her, leaving behind a household of belongings. Genevieve told me that they would go to Venice and then take the train to her mother's home in the French countryside. I couldn't wait to see her, but I was in Germany, so why was she going to France? I didn't understand. She explained that she couldn't see me for three weeks, having promised the base commander. "Impossible!" I declared, "I want to come and see you now." I wanted us to be together for our tenth anniversary in a few days and to spend Christmas together. She said, "No, no, I gave my word, and the arrangements have been made." I was so thrilled to know they were free that I didn't notice the strain in her voice.

I was not satisfied with Genevieve's explanation, and I wanted more information.

I called the consulate in Stuttgart, but they knew nothing about the conditions surrounding my wife and son's release. I called Bill, but he didn't know anything about the arrangement. Nor did Dr. Mason. The base officials had not given Genevieve anything in writing, so I had to take her word for it. I did, but it was very difficult to accept.

A few days later Genevieve called to say she was sending Eric to Germany to be with me. I got us settled in an attic apartment on base and enrolled him in the eleventh grade. Oh, it was so wonderful to see him, but I missed Genevieve terribly. She had said that she hoped to join us in a few weeks, but I couldn't wait. I made arrangements for someone to look in on Eric, and I took off for France. I arrived at her mother's in the middle of the night. While I was thrilled to take Genevieve in my arms, she was very upset. First, I had left Eric alone. And second, she had promised the base officials that she wouldn't see me so soon. Summarily, she sent me back to Germany.

I didn't realize it at the time, but she needed an adjustment period after the harrowing three months she had been at Wheelus. When she recounted her experiences later, I understood completely.

So, I returned to Germany, having been away for less than twenty-four hours. Eric was fine, and we spent a good three weeks together. In early January Genevieve joined us, but she was still going through a readjustment phase. She was quiet and reserved, as someone who had been traumatized.

I went about my work for Dr. Mason in the district office. One day he heard word that Libyan agents in Germany might be looking for me. He suggested things were a little too "hot" for me there, and proposed, "Dan, you and your family should leave Germany." I concurred, "Whatever you say, Doc. You have been so supportive, I'll do as you advise." Dr. Mason continued, "I'm going to send you to Washington to work at the Pentagon, recruiting teachers for our school system. You'll maintain your pay grade and receive a housing allowance. I'll have your furnishings stored here until you're ready for them." I was very grateful for this generous offer.

DoDDS issued orders for us to depart for the States in a few days. Before we left, our furniture arrived from Libya. What a mess! It was obvious that the GIs who packed for us were not professional packers, nor did they care how our belongings were handled. Maybe they'd been told I was a troublemaker. Everything was thrown into three shipping containers in a jumble. With only a few days to go, I frantically worked day and night to put our things in order. A German packing company assisted me, and they did a beautiful job. Perhaps they were sympathetic, having heard about my circumstances.

On the Saturday of our departure, a full colonel and his driver were assigned to escort our family through the final preparation for our departure. The military sedan took us from Karlsruhe to Heidelberg where the army finance office opened especially for the purpose of providing me with a TDY advance for travel expenses. From there we were driven to Frankfurt's U.S. military airport, where the colonel ensured that we boarded the flight and departed without incident.

I was never given the reasons for this special treatment, but surmised that Dr. Mason was looking out for my safety regarding fallout from the Libya incident, while also being pressured by the U.S. military to get me out of Europe.

EIGHT

Recovering in D.C. and Okinawa

We moved into an apartment on the bus line in Arlington from where I could easily commute to the Department of Defense Overseas School System offices in the basement of the Pentagon. This was in early February of 1970.

After a few months the trauma of the recent past began to recede. Genevieve located a good riding club near Mt. Vernon, a considerable distance from where we lived. It was a long ride by bus, but the results were worthwhile for her recovery process. She rode horses again and met new friends with common interests. Settling into this new environment, she felt more like herself. Gradually, she told me of her and Eric's experiences on base. Her stories made my ears curl.

The day I left Libya, no one knew the real reason for my trip to Malta, except Genevieve. She also knew the plane was scheduled to return that evening. When she learned of the delay caused by the storm, she expected my return the following day, so she wasn't worried. The next morning, the police arrived at our house on the base. They pounded on the door and barged in angrily, saying, "We're here to search the house. Save us a lot of trouble and tell us where the money is!" "What money?" was Genevieve's perplexed reply. The investigators spoke harshly, "We have your husband in custody in Malta for illegally escorting someone out of Libya for money. Save us the trouble by telling us where the money is and we won't tear your house apart."

Now frightened for herself, as well as concerned about my welfare, she maintained composure and gave her honest answer, "Well, there is no money here. You can look all you want, but there's no money around. The only thing I have is this statement that my husband left, which gives the reason why he did it."

"We're going to look anyway." And they went about searching the house from top to bottom, rummaging around the bedroom and bathroom and looking behind the toilets and in the desk. They took my collection of calling cards I had collected from the many special visitors we had entertained in our home. Perhaps they thought my social connections would somehow serve as evidence against me. The Office of Security Investigation, or OSI, was still not convinced and soon returned to search the house for a second time. Even after Genevieve provided my written statement, the house was turned upside-down for a third time. Upon their departure, the OSI ordered Genevieve to not leave the house under any circumstances. She was unofficially on house arrest and being treated as an accessory to a crime!

The many Americans on base with whom we were acquainted began to avoid her. She had very few visitors, and no one phoned. The principal's wife visited occasionally and a few neighbors checked on her. Two American women in particular went out of their way to befriend Genevieve once they realized that for all intents and purposes she was being held prisoner in her home. Some Libyan custodians came by to bring fresh fruit and inquire about us. It was so kind of them. One of our Arab friends checked to see how Genevieve was doing. In that era, Arabs and Americans were on amicable terms, and our respective countries did not have any contentious issues with politics, religion, or threat of violence.

After a few days, the base commander had a colonel from Criminal Investigation Division, or CID, bring Genevieve to his office for a serious discussion. The commander told her that I was being held in jail and she had better confess the whole thing in order to help her situation. She said there was nothing to confess, and she handed him my written statement, reiterating, "It was a humanitarian act that he did, and I have nothing more to say." To further complicate matters, the personal letter I'd given to the military pilot in Malta for delivery to Genevieve was given directly to the base commander upon landing at Wheelus! After the meeting between the base commander and Genevieve, the CID colonel told her in confidence that the commander was over-stating the situation, as I was not in a Maltese jail, but in fact, safe in Germany. This colonel was very kind to my wife, helpfully informing her of her rights and the availability of legal assistance.

Genevieve did not sleep for a whole week after receiving news of my detainment. She heard all kinds of noises at night. Restless and on edge, the slightest disturbance caused her alarm. By the bed she kept a Spanish Toreador sword, purchased in Spain on one of our trips. This gave her a feeling of some security, although the commander's scare tactics had her agonizing with fear. She didn't want to cause Eric distress and suffered in silence while keeping a brave exterior. She saw him off to school every day and prepared him dinner every night, as if nothing were out of the ordinary.

On one occasion the base commander sent an ambulance over to our home, claiming he'd heard she was ill. Asserting she should go to the hospital to get an examination, he suggested she rest there for a few days. Genevieve wisely refused. "No, there is nothing wrong with me," she told the paramedics. She sensed it was a ruse to create worrisome news and bait me. Believe me, the commander was clever because his ploy for my return would have worked if I thought Genevieve was actually ill.

When Eric did not return home from school one day, Genevieve was frantic with worry. She called around and was unable to find news of him. Later that evening he came home, telling her that he'd stopped off to watch a basketball game nearby. This was not an unusual thing for a fifteen-year old to do, but under the circumstances it was cause for high anxiety.

The commander sent for her again, this time threatening to hand her over to the Libyans if I didn't turn myself in. He then tried to terrorize her by saying that Arab radicals were coming after her! But she held her ground. I can picture this tall, intimidating authority bullying a petite, dignified Frenchwoman as she bravely faced him in his office and commented that his swearing was unbecoming an officer of his rank and position. He bellowed, "You're pushing me, Mrs. DeCarlo, you're pushing me." The CID colonel who was both the driver and a witness to Genevieve's meetings with the commander later complimented Genevieve, saying he was quite proud of the way she handled herself.

The next time the commander threatened Genevieve, he said he'd turn her over to the Libyans for interrogation and provide a translator from the base on her behalf. Anticipating another of his tricks, Genevieve said she'd comply, but she noted that she didn't require a translator because she could communicate quite well in the language. This shook him up, as he did not know of Genevieve's language skills. Interrogation wasn't brought up again.

If all this weren't enough, Genevieve began getting phone calls from an anonymous heavy breather. When no one spoke, she asked, "Who is this? Hello, hello?" All she heard was heavy breathing that continued until she hung up. It was most unsettling for her. This happened a few times, as Genevieve always felt compelled to pick up the phone in case it was Eric saying he'd be delayed. She reported these incidents to the next door neighbor, a major, who had a friend in the telephone exchange. His friend agreed to tap the phone. If it happened again, she was instructed to keep the line open as long as possible. Sure enough it happened again, so she kept asking, "Who are you? What do you want? Why are you calling here?" The telephone people were listening in on the line as they completed the trace and Genevieve overheard them gasp, "Oh my God, it's the commander's house!" The major was furious, and apparently word got back to the CID colonel, who assured Genevieve that the phone harassment would stop, which it did.

The neighborhood where we lived on base had a mix of officers and enlisted personnel. On several occasions, bottles and beer cans were thrown over the fence into our yard. These were acts of vandalism, targeted at us.

Bill briefly visited Genevieve and Eric at Wheelus and observed the security measures implemented by the CID colonel's office by orders from the commander. Guards were stationed at the house in shifts, day and night. The overnight guard found it hard to stay awake and usually fell asleep in our comfortable living room chair. On the occasions when Genevieve had permission to leave the house, a guard always accompanied her. The pretense of the commander's order was to protect my family from a purported threat of Libyan soldiers stationed outside the base gates. I'm sure it was actually to prevent my family's escape, as if a housewife and her teenaged son were some sort of cunning counter-spies! The conscientious CID colonel was following the commander's orders by posting guards, but the judicious result, as he intended, was to ensure their protection.

Without any communication between the two of us, Genevieve anticipated all our possible losses, including many worst-case scenarios that must have kept her tossing and turning at night, planning for an uncertain future. Although not permitted to receive or send any mail, she did so secretly. Rather than using her name or return address, her two new American sympathizers and a few other trusted friends used their names and addresses to covertly aid her in sending out some thirty-eight boxes of our valuables through the Wheelus post office to be held safely by our friends and family all over Europe and the States. The shipments included cherished photos, our set of heirloom silverware, and some of our important papers—things she felt we would probably lose.

***

My assignment in D.C. was in the Office of Dependent Education to help with recruiting new teachers for the overseas school system. There were three recruiters, representing the Atlantic, Pacific, and European areas. I was in charge of the European area, which needed about 1,800 teachers. I reviewed applications and filed them by grade and subject area. We had about 20,000 applications from teachers all over the U.S. We did not interview the teachers, as traveling recruiters performed this function. When we received personnel requests from our respective directors' offices, we'd do the research to find an applicant who met the qualifications. The work was tedious at times, but I found it very interesting to review all the applications and talk with so many teachers.

Our office supervisor was an authoritative woman of imposing dimensions. I observed how she relegated certain applicants' folders to a "reject" pile, and wondered if she was following orders or acting on her own. It took great effort for me to mask my disappointment with the hiring system as certain characteristics of those rejected became clear to me. Applications from those with big families were set aside, likely because it was costlier to relocate and house them. Ironically, overweight applicants had low priority, as well. I won't even speculate on the reasons for this. Applicants who had attended particular colleges that were known for providing scholarships to the underprivileged were also shuffled. Among the other undesirables were retired military personnel, especially officers because they tended to question the system.

The most highly desirable demographic was young single women. One overseas school director, a husband and father, was a notorious ladies' man. He requested the transfer of a particular female teacher by name and insisted that we find a position for her under his jurisdiction. Our office complied. After all the trouble I'd stirred up before my transfer to the Pentagon, I thought it best that I keep a low profile and be just a little cog in the wheel. Eventually, however, I did have a serious run-in with this dallying director.

The single teachers could be economically housed in the BOQ, or Bachelor Officers' Quarters. The unspoken reason for this high demand, however, was probably their contribution to morale among the single men on base. I knew this firsthand from my two years as supervising principal at Wheelus, where the pilots would anxiously ask me months ahead when the new teachers

were expected. The antics of young singles on base are foresee-
able, especially when they're in close proximity to each other in
an isolated area of an Arab country. In one instance of which I'm
aware, a pilot moved in with a teacher who had moved out of
the BOQ. The colonel in charge was concerned with appearances
and asked me to tell the teacher in question to be more discreet.
I was incensed at this double standard and countered, "If you'll
speak to your pilots about being more discreet, then I'll talk to
the teachers about being more discreet with their indiscretions."

My job at the Pentagon was temporary until I could secure
work in the schools as before. Eight months into our Washington
transfer, we were informed that my Libya controversy might still
be too recent for us to return to Europe. The Pacific area had
availability for the next school year, however, and that sounded
quite promising.

Genevieve signed up for Japanese studies at the Japanese Cultural Center and made friends there. Our new friends invited
us to parties, including a reception to honor William Rogers,
Secretary of State in the Nixon administration. We accepted the
invitation with some trepidation, as we were concerned that security personnel knew about all the grief I had caused the State
Department.

It was a lovely black-tie affair, and Genevieve was radiant in
her elegant gown. I was nervous as we approached the reception
desk, but the woman recognized Genevieve and just waved us on
without looking at the guest list. Security people were all over the
place, and if they'd checked my record, we probably would not
have been admitted. We mingled with some other high-ranking
officials and met Secretary Rogers. We chatted a few minutes,
and I told him I was working at the Pentagon for the overseas
school system. He commented on Genevieve's accent and spoke
to her with a few words in French. Little did he realize who we
were, what I had done, and how much trouble I had given his
department six months earlier. Although I must admit I did not
have a good opinion of his department, he was a very congenial

and pleasant person. It was a thoroughly enjoyable evening and one of the best parties we attended in Washington.

Eric was enrolled in a nearby high school. He came home after the first day saying he was asked several times if he wanted to buy pot, which took him quite by surprise. This wasn't something he'd experienced in the overseas schools. Eric was resilient through our many relocations, a real trooper. He settled in, did his studies, got a job at the local Burger Chef, and saved his money to buy a car when he was old enough. I promised to match his savings.

We were enjoying ourselves in Washington. We visited all the sights we could: the presidential monuments, Mt. Vernon, the galleries, and the Smithsonian, again and again! The springtime cherry blossoms were spectacular. My coworker lent me his car, so we were able to tour the surrounding areas and see Virginia's green countryside.

At the office, we had filled most of the vacancies in the schools, and my temporary job was winding down. When discussion began regarding my next assignment, I was offered work with the Indian reservation schools in the U.S. This sounded like an attempt to railroad me out of DoDDS and the work I wanted to continue. If I accepted the position, I'd have to resign from government service and enter the public sector, which is probably what they wanted. It wasn't what I wanted, and I knew they couldn't fire me, as my rights were legally protected. Instead of discussing resignation I indicated that I wanted to remain with DoDDS. In response, it was suggested that I go to the Pacific area where it was "safer" for me. Perhaps it was seen as less likely that I would cause a political scandal there.

I researched schools in Okinawa and found an administrative vacancy at Kubasaki High, a modern 2,000-student school for grades ten through twelve. Being that I was in a position to assign personnel, I promptly assigned myself to that job. It was one of the best decisions I ever made. Although it was a downgrade to a GS-11 level, the contract was guaranteed. Dr. Mason agreed to the transfer, telling me I could return to Europe in a few years when things cooled off.

Once I received my orders, we packed for relocation to Japan. I was given concurrent travel with my family, an unusual benefit. Surprisingly, our household shipping did not have a weight limit. This worked to our advantage as we had a full 11,000 pounds of household goods. Clearly they wanted me in Okinawa. And so began a new adventure.

Life doesn't always go as smoothly as we wish. Our bus to Travis Air Force Base was caught in snarled traffic, so we missed our flight and had to stay overnight in the base BOQ. I called the school director in Okinawa and informed him I'd arrive late. We boarded the plane the next day but we had to land in Guam due to bad weather in Okinawa. Another call was made to the director and another day lost in getting to our destination. We inquired for a room in the BOQ, but they could not accommodate a family, so we ended up at a hotel near the school.

While staying through that stormy night in Guam, I worried with anticipation that these delays were an indication of things to come.

***

At the start of the school year in 1970 we settled easily into life on the U.S. base of Fort Buckner on the island of Okinawa and I found Kubasaki High to be a beautiful school on an attractive campus. My new boss, John Weldon, had been my colleague at Verona Elementary in Italy some eleven years prior. He and his staff really set the tone for a new beginning for me in Kubasaki. Not only did I flourish, but under the capable direction of Mr. Weldon as principal, Kubasaki went from being a good school to an excellent school. While all my overseas assignments were invaluable, I considered Kubasaki High School as one of the best.

Indeed, my luck was changing. When the assistant principal, a GS-12, transferred to another school, Weldon recommended me as a permanent replacement to fill the vacancy. When I received the promotion, there was a surprise benefit for me by way of a loophole in the system. It went like this: if a GS-12 downgrades to a GS-11 to fill a needed position and then goes back to a GS-12, regulations required a two-level upgrade from the previous one. This put me at the top of the GS-12 pay scale and two steps up, instead of having to wait four years for that upgrade under normal circumstances. What a lucky break! I was very grateful that I had kept my standing with DoDDS and secured the number two position at the school.

As vice principal, I was in charge of personnel, maintenance, supplies, and curriculum. It was a big responsibility and I gladly took on the challenge. I admit that I might not have been the brightest bulb in the room but I applied every effort to being organized and efficient. My philosophy was that well-supplied teachers are happy teachers, and happy teachers make happy students who want to learn. The reason we are educators is to help students learn, and the process should be fun!

The faculty at Kubasaki High was exceptional. It consisted of caring, experienced teachers from various backgrounds. Under the direction of Bill Hobbs, our yearbook and newspaper staff produced an all-American yearbook and newspaper that won many national awards. Giacomo "Jock" Leone ran our outstanding drama department. Their productions could match those of any large high school or college in the U.S. As the only American high school on the island, our athletic department sponsored intramural sports. We fielded four complete football teams, five basketball teams, track, wrestling, and more. The marching band and the orchestra, in the capable hands of Dan Mitchum, were top notch.

The Business Education Department, comprised of six teachers, thrived under the direction of Lois Shook, one of the original teachers who taught on front porches before school buildings were constructed. Lois was also bookkeeper for student funds. She was so thorough and meticulous that finance officers throughout the Pacific area recommended that all schools follow her procedures. Ms. Nestaval, a great asset to the school, directed the English Department. The Foreign Language Department was also superb, as we were one of the few public high schools to offer Latin, French, German, Spanish, and Japanese.

Joanna James headed Social Studies, and Harold Bickley led the Math Department. Harold pioneered the first computer education program in Pacific-area high schools. Remember when computers ran on reel-to-reel tapes? They were terribly slow, but they got the job done. Harold, technologically progressive, acquired fifty computers for student use. Doug Dorman expanded the Industrial Arts Department into a work/study lab, thus giving a head start to many students who desired trade skills. Our art department, with four teachers under the direction of Dottie Norton, encouraged students to be creative. I thought the artwork was so well done that I bought a number of pieces as gifts for our friends in Europe. I wish I could name all the wonderful teachers and staff during the fourteen years I was at Kubasaki, but space and time do not permit me to do so. Let me just say how much I enjoyed working with a staff who knew what and how to teach.

After living in a hotel for three months, we relocated to on-base housing. This was much more economical and convenient. All told, we were doing well. Genevieve's health was improving, and Eric excelled in school. With money he had earned working at Burger Chef in Virginia, Eric bought a snazzy, red, second-hand convertible Honda. It needed some fixing, but he went to work on it and in no time was driving it around. After our first year at Kubasaki, Eric graduated from high school in the class of '71 and went to Florida Institute of Technology, or FIT. Genevieve and I were very proud of him, but we also had to adjust to life as empty nesters.

My early years at Kubasaki marked the beginning of exchange programs between Japanese students and our American army base students. At first the programs involved high schools in mainland Japan. Eventually, the programs were expanded to include schools on Okinawa. Of interest, Okinawa didn't consider

Eric's first car

itself to be part of Japan, and it had a long history of contention with the mainland.

This cultural exchange was an amazing experience. During these enriching visits, our students, staying in the homes of their Japanese counterparts, learned many interesting things about the Japanese people and culture, far beyond what could be learned from books. Some of the American and Japanese students remained in contact for years afterwards.

There were certainly differences in lifestyles. Some of our students, allowed to smoke on campus at Kubasaki, had to surrender their packs of cigarettes to customs upon arrival at airports on mainland Japan. Japanese students were not permitted to have cigarettes in their possession at school, so the American students had to forfeit theirs.

Genevieve and I also participated in the programs, such as the one with Kagoshima High on the mainland. The school was about 1,500 miles away and nearly a three-hour flight from the base at Okinawa. At Kagoshima, every one of the 4,000 students took off their shoes and put on slippers before entering the school and walking on the wood floors. In fact, everyone entering the school was expected to remove their shoes according to custom since there were no janitors. School went into session at seven A.M. At ten A.M. when a bell rang, all the students went to work cleaning the school from top to bottom, including offices, restrooms, classrooms, and hallways. The students were organized and completely engrossed in their work. I've never seen anything like it in any of the countries I've lived or visited.

On this particular trip, Mr. Sanada, the Kagoshima High principal, invited the American teachers for after-dinner drinks at a Geisha restaurant where the doll-like women danced for us in their ornate kimonos. The sake flowed generously, yet no one overindulged, and we had a fantastic evening with our kind hosts.

We also accepted, with some trepidation, an invitation to experience the public bath. I was uncomfortable with the idea of men and women bathing together, but as we approached the building I was relieved to see separate entrances. There was a scale in the men's bath where everyone weighed in. Judging by their surprised exclamations of "Ah, so!" the Japanese men were apparently impressed that I tipped the scale at 200 pounds.

Genevieve and I became friends with Mr. Sanada and his petite, charmingly traditional wife. On our visits to their home, we slept on a tatami mat with a wooden block for a pillow. My neck had a crick from the hard "pillow," so on the second night of our stay I rolled up my pajama top as padding for the tortuous headrest. Still, I complimented Mrs. Sanada for her gracious hospitality, as she made every effort to ensure our comfort in their modest home. I commented to Mr. Sanada on how efficient, pleasant, caring, and thoughtful his wife was. He replied, with much insight, "Yes, she is pre-war."

While the Japanese students were intent on learning English, our Kubasaki students and staff spoke very little, if any, Japanese. That is, except for Genevieve, who acted as our translator on many occasions. I believe that experiencing the customs, language, and culture of another country brings a deeper understanding of the world and humanity as a whole, creating fewer misunderstandings and reducing the likelihood of wars.

Genevieve was hired by the local university to teach French and English. In the process she befriended many students, who we invited to our home to join us in celebrating various French and American holidays. An interesting Japanese custom was the high regard they held for their sensei, or teachers. If you mention that you're a teacher, or when a teacher enters a classroom, the young people stand and bow several times to show their respect. This is quite a contrast to the behavior of western students, as in the U.S. teaching is considered to be just another job.

*** *** ***

Okinawa was wonderful, but in our hearts we desired to return to France someday. A year after our transfer to Japan, Genevieve traveled to France to attend her mother's funeral. When the estate was settled, Genevieve and her four siblings each received the equivalent of $4,000 that Genevieve wished to invest in our dream, a home in France where we could retire. The following summer we went back to France to look at properties and were instantly enamored by Le Quanty, a fifteenth-century manor house on beautiful acreage with grazing livestock. We bought the gorgeous property under an agreement that gave us immediate access to a sizable portion of the huge seventeen-room home while the owners, two elderly sisters, lived out their lives in another section of the house. Per French law we were to be deeded full ownership when they both passed away.

As we envisioned our future, we planned not only to retire to Le Quanty, but also to create and run a "Center for Intercultural Exchange," or CIE, for young people there. Every summer we traveled to France to bring life to our concept, and we made a considerable investment in bringing the manor up-to-date. We put new roofs on the manor itself, as well as the two barns, installed plumbing and electricity, added heating, built a staircase, moved

Our CIE flag was rich with symbolism

interior walls, updated the flooring, and much more. With these improvements completed, soon we were hosting students from Japan, England, Canada, Kuwait, and the U.S. every summer. Our exchange students enjoyed touring the French countryside and seeing the sights, as well as sharing the differences and similarities in their languages and cultures. These interactions enriched everyone involved. The CIE flag I designed incorporated colors and motifs shared by all humanity, including the earth, sun, stars, moon, the blue sky, and the red blood that flows through our veins, men and women alike. I loved this concept and its early success on a small scale, so I drew up plans to expand the facilities to accommodate a larger number of guests by transforming the large barns into dorms. To this end, I created a booklet describing our goals for the center and contacted philanthropic foundations requesting their sponsorship for expansion. While a few prospects for investors looked promising, nothing materialized.

NINE

Fighting the System

I enjoyed the feelings of accomplishment and productivity from my hard work at Kubasaki High. I felt that I knew the system and how to work with the military to get things done for the benefit of the students and staff. I received step increases and cash awards for my efforts, cooperated with leadership, and kept my record clean as I had promised Dr. Mason. I even resisted publishing my traumatic Libya experiences, which I wanted very much to do!

After ten years in Japan, Genevieve and I were finding it difficult to manage our student exchange project in France while living in Japan most of the year. It was time to initiate the process of securing a transfer to Europe. Over the next two years I submitted numerous requests through the system, and observed with frustration that other administrators were granted transfers for Europe. But it wasn't happening for me and I began to question the fairness of the system to which I had dedicated my life. I had to make a decision on how to proceed.

On one hand, I recalled the success I had in 1960 in Verona, when I questioned the faulty repair work that was done to keep rain from pouring in when opening classroom doors. To make changes, I followed the DoD procedures and suggested a new design, which was subsequently approved and implemented. Despite my success, the school principal thoughtfully advised me not to suggest changes if I wanted to get ahead in the system. I never forgot his sage advice, and held back my comments over the years while observing unbelievably wasteful spending on materials, repairs, and new construction. I wanted to be a team player and I learned that to get along I had to go along.

On the other hand, I had received advice some years earlier from an experienced administrator whose philosophy was to "Give 'em hell." The premise was that if you irritate those in charge enough, they would move you out of the way and out of the district. To get out of the limbo in which I was stuck, I decided to give this route a try. I dared to question the system, which lead to the third major crisis in our lives.

I was aware that my regional director was abusing the Environmental Morale Leave, or EML, system. Civilian employees and their families were allowed two trips out of Okinawa each year, but the director's wife enjoyed seven to ten annual trips to exotic destinations. While she was away, he carried on with a number of women. After the director promoted his good friend to the position I had requested in Europe, a job for which he was not qualified, I anonymously blew the whistle on the director for his wife's excessive travel at huge taxpayer's expense. After an investigation proved me correct, he had to pay back over $3,000 and was hopping mad. He asked me point-blank if I was the one who reported him. I answered, "Do you think I'm stupid?" Of course, I would never admit my involvement, but I'm sure he never stopped suspecting me.

Following procedures, I filed a complaint through the inspector general's office without fear of reprisal, as was my right. I charged that the director of the transfer program had discriminated against me in overlooking my transfer requests. As part of the process, I was required to present my case to the director himself and a personnel officer. To prepare, I asked a teacher from another school to assist and represent me. This teacher happened to be the leader of the teacher's union, of which I was a member.

On the day of the meeting my representative and I waited in the conference room before the others arrived. When the director and the personnel officer entered and noted my representative, they turned around and walked out in a huff, asking, "What is HE doing here?" I simply replied that he was my representative. We waited a little while, so I could present my complaint. Upon their return the director explained that my situation was out of his hands, but he indicated that they would look into it. I took notes on the discussion, and we left with no ill will.

After several anxious weeks, I finally received the letter that I had thought would speed my transfer. Instead, it shook me to my core. The powers in charge accused me of violating the relationship between the administration and the union by having the union leader as my representative. I was to be terminated from my job as a GS-12 assistant principal immediately. I couldn't believe this devastating news. I was actually getting fired from my job! I had set out to rock the boat a little, but now it appeared I was sinking the ship.

The next day the superintendent of schools explained that I was not to be fired, but rather demoted to teach fifth grade on mainland Japan. Orders were being cut for me to leave in two days. With the gravity of my situation weighing on me, I wrote an open letter to friends and family, as follows:

June 18, 1982
Subj: Daniel A. DeCarlo

1. Mr. Daniel A. DeCarlo, age 52, is presently employed by the Department of Defense Dependent Schools as assistant principal at Kubasaki High School on Okinawa. He has been a DoDDS employee for 24 years and has received a number of awards for creditable service. He received a Commendable Performance rating for the 1981-82 school year from his immediate supervisor, Mr. Joe Jerick, Principal GS-13 of Kubasaki High School. Mr. DeCarlo's present rating is GS-12.

2. On May 24, 1982, Mr. DeCarlo received a letter of proposed removal signed by the Education Program Administrator for DoDDS-Pacific, allegedly for violations of federal service labor/management relations statute and DoD policy and conflict of interest. Specifically, it was alleged that Mr. DeCarlo "flagrantly violated" federal law and

DoD policy by being represented by the area representative and by using legal counsel of the Overseas Education Association in equal opportunity complaints Mr. DeCarlo filed against DoDDS-Pacific.

3. Immediately upon receipt of the letter of proposed removal, Mr. DeCarlo, who was unaware that his association with the Overseas Education Association was contrary to established policy or directives, withdrew his membership in the organization and, as required, answered the letter of proposed removal on May 27, 1982, explaining that he had been neither counseled or warned of any improprieties even though the DoDDS-Pacific and Washington administration had been aware of his association with the organization since April 1, 1981. Mr. DeCarlo also stated in his letter that he considered the action unduly severe.

4. The letter of proposed removal stated that Mr. DeCarlo, in his present position, was responsible for the day-to-day administration of provisions of the Federal Labor/Management Relations statute relating to the OEA as an organization and to bargaining unit members represented by the OEA. Mr. DeCarlo was an associate member of the organization and has never engaged in bargaining matters with OEA. At no time prior to the issuance of the supervisor's letter was Mr. DeCarlo warned that his association with that organization may be in violation of DoD policy. All his contacts with the organization were strictly for legal advice concerning equal opportunity complaints filed by him against the Director's office.

5. On June 8, 1982, the Director reviewing Mr. DeCarlo's reclaimer to the letter of proposed removal, removed Mr. DeCarlo from his position as assistant principal GS-12 of Kubasaki High School and demoted him to the position of teacher, Class I, Category 105 (fifth grade) as of August 15, 1982.

6. *In Mr. DeCarlo's opinion, the action taken by the Supervisor constitutes a reprisal for Mr. DeCarlo's filing of EEO & IG complaints against the Supervisor. Those complaints detailed what Mr. DeCarlo sincerely believed to be incidence of fraud and abuse committed by the Director. Mr. DeCarlo believes the action taken by the Supervisor to be tantamount to removal from the DoDDS system entirely since Mr. DeCarlo has not taught in a classroom for more than 20 years and, consequently, is no longer fully qualified to do so. His demotion is not in the best interests of the students he will be assigned to teach and is unduly severe in that it will result in his salary being cut approximately in half, causing extreme hardship for Mr. DeCarlo and his family.*

7. *While there is an appeal system through which Mr. DeCarlo can seek to have this harsh and severe action reversed, using that system could take months or years at Mr. DeCarlo's expense, while the Supervisor will have the full resources of the U.S. Government and the comparatively unlimited taxpayer's funding at his disposal. Mr. DeCarlo considers the action by the Supervisor to be contrived to remove him from the DoDDS-Pacific system in retaliation for his allegations of fraud and abuse by the Director.*
8. *Mr. DeCarlo is asking that the demotion action against him be held in abeyance and that he be allowed to remain in his present position until an impartial investigation by parties outside the influence of DoDDS can be conducted.*

9. *As a responsible citizen and a federal employee paid by the American taxpayers, it was Mr. DeCarlo's duty to bring to the attention of appropriate authorities instances of apparent fraud and abuse perpetrated by federal officials. For him to be punished by the very official against whom such complaints were lodged reeks of revenge and further abuse of authority.*

10. Even if Mr. DeCarlo did violate federal regulations by his association with the OEA, it would appear that the most equitable solution would have been to apprise him of his wrongdoing and give him reasonable opportunity to correct the situation. It is emphasized that the officials now taking unduly severe punitive action against Mr. DeCarlo were aware for a considerable period of time of Mr. DeCarlo's association with that organization. That they are taking this action now, after his filing of EEO complaints, is further evidence of revenge and abuse of authority.

11. This is only the latest of a number of incidents of punishment of "whistle-blowers" by the superiors, which have been publicized over the last year. A thorough impartial investigation into this case will reveal that Mr. DeCarlo is a victim of the abuse of power rather than a violator of DoDDS policy.

Your kind assistance and attention to this matter would prevent a gross injustice from being committed.

Further information may be obtained from:
Daniel A. DeCarlo
Assistant Principal KHS

I knew I had a valid case, but I desperately needed professional help. I pulled out a ten-year old Washington D.C. phone book, flipped through the yellow page listings of 300 law firms, and let my finger pick a name at random. It was literally like playing Pin-the-Tail-on-the-Donkey.

I phoned the number and asked to speak with a lawyer who could help me with a labor dispute involving the government. My call was transferred, and a young lawyer by the name of Joseph Kolick answered. I gave him a quick summary of my case, and he caught everything I said, including the fact that I only had two days before being removed from my position! Despite the short time frame, he was calm and reassuring. I was concerned about his fees, but he told me that we'd deal with the fees later. In the meantime, he needed to get busy right away and make some calls.

I spent a very long day, worrying and waiting for him to call me back. During the course of twelve hours, he succeeded in obtaining a stay order from the special counsel, preventing any further action. This, in essence, delayed my demotion and transfer to Japan until a hearing could be held. He instructed me not to do or say anything and said his letter containing details was on its way. It was amazing! This lawyer seemed to be a miracle worker. I spoke to no one about my new strategy, except for Genevieve.

Later that day the assistant superintendent called to confirm that orders had been cut for me to leave in two days and suggested I start packing for departure. He indicated that Genevieve could join me at the new assignment later. All I did was thank him for the information. Meantime, word got out, from whom I do not know, that I was suddenly being transferred. Many teachers called and stopped by my office to inquire, but I couldn't discuss the matter although I knew I wasn't going anywhere soon.

The assistant superintendent again called me at home to give me flight information. He stressed that I needed to be on that plane for the noon takeoff the next day. Either he had not heard from the special counsel or maybe he had and was pushing me. I was as pleasant as could be.

On the day of departure, the superintendent called two hours before I was to board the plane to explain that I was granted a stay by the special counsel. I gave a surprised "Oh?" He further stated I would retain my GS-12 position until a hearing had been held.

About a week later I received a letter from Kolick outlining the case he had put together. Genevieve had brought the mail to me at my office and held out the envelope he had sent. She remarked, "This looks like good news." Sure enough, he had put together an airtight case that saved us a huge amount of anxiety and distress. He stated that my rights had been violated and my removal further violated established procedures and civil service regulations. He tersely said DoDDS had treated me in an unconscionable manner, and concluded with, "and that's putting it charitably." What a relief! There seemed to be hope! I couldn't believe how fortunate I was to have chosen Kolick from pages and pages of attorney listings. My finger stopped at the right page and at the right name among hundreds. Call it what you may, but somebody was guiding that hand!

The hearing finally took place several months later at considerable taxpayer expense. I estimate the proceedings cost about $200,000 considering the investigators' time spent collecting hundreds of pages of depositions and testimonies, as well as their lodging, meals, temporary duty assignment, or TDY, airfares and other transportation costs. Much time, too, had been taken away from our school staff's valuable work hours. I was, of course, responsible for my own attorney's fees, which were surprisingly reasonable considering the results. My total cost was only a few thousand dollars, a bit less than a month's pay.

In the end, the special counsel made their determination as follows:

> There is no evidence that DeCarlo took an affirmative stance against management and in favor of the union in any activities. Although the Notice of Removal stated that DeCarlo was responsible for administrating labor relations, it appears DeCarlo had no actual responsibility for negotiations for dealing with the union in his position as assistant principal. There is no evidence of conflict of interest. The agency is unlikely to show it had a legitimate reason for its actions. The board extends for ninety days the proposed demotion and reassignment of Daniel DeCarlo.

To our great relief, I had been released from the false accusation of inappropriately working with the teacher's union. Throughout this period I had worried so much, as had Genevieve, whose kind nature meant that she, too, suffered when I suffered. I had never again wanted to put her through anything like our terrible ordeal in Libya. I wrote the following letter to

Kolick, and it is included in this section because it will give you an overall view of the dilemmas I faced.

21 January 83
Mr. Joseph Kolick
2101 L Street, N.W.
Washington, D.C.

Dear Joe,

I would like to convey the events of my proposed removal from federal service and to express my thoughts and feelings about them. Perhaps this will give you an idea how I feel.

The overall thought which crosses my mind time and time again is how can such severe action be taken on allegations only before a hearing or review by a third party? To me, this is un-American and strikes at a very fundamental principle that a person is "innocent until proven guilty." I was to be moved, downgraded and punished before a hearing was conducted.

The Director of DoDDS-Pacific was not treated this way. There was an allegation or charge of fraud and abuse of the EML Program by his dependent. There was an extensive, almost eight month investigation, before any action was taken against this person. He was not punished before it was proven he abused the system. Why, then, was I punished before an investigation was conducted? Why was I to be moved, lose over $18,000 in salary, lose position, rank, status and etc., before an investigation or hearing was conducted? This is difficult for me to believe this double standard exists.

The same double standard was applied to another director last March, he was moved from his position for some unknown reason (although the rumors have it for kickbacks and conflict of interest). He was moved from one office to another without loss of pay. I am positive he was moved after there was an investigation and not before.

Again, it appears a double standard exists for upper level GS employees and one for the lower level GS employees, such as myself. How can this happen or be permitted to happen in our system of government? My Japanese landlord, when I tried to explain why I might have to move, stated, "Is this the way your American democracy works?" Do we really have equal justice under the law?

A great injustice would have taken place if it had not been for your good efforts and the efforts of a special counsel. The fact that so much energy, time and effort had to be exerted to have justice done, or simply put, to have a hearing before the punishment to see if the allegations were true. This was all I asked for and begged for, "Don't punish me until you find out if I was wrong!" Instead, the Director of DoDDS stated, "It is DoD and the school policy not to delay imposition of discipline pending the outcome of the grievance or appeal." In other words you are guilty until proven innocent. The Director continues to state, "After you are punished, moved, downgraded, etc., you may appeal and possibly win your case. If you win, you will be reinstated in your previous position without loss of pay." The Director does not take into consideration the agony, the hardship and suffering one goes through to be downgraded, disgraced, moved out of his home, loss of $18,000 in pay, and moved to a classroom teaching position. I haven't taught in twenty years. They were not thinking of the best interest of the students or me in that assignment.

It appears that I will win my case, but can the Director restore what this action has cost me in human endeavor? Can he restore the joy I missed of not being able to attend a family reunion with my mother on her 80th birthday? Can the Director restore that occasion? Can the Director restore the joy and happiness missed by parents, waiting for their son to receive his doctorate degree? We have waited 10 years for that occasion, only to be missed because of the Director's allegations that I broke federal law and his refusal to permit me to go home, unless I first moved to Japan. Can the Directors restore that happy occasion? Can the Director restore the cost in delaying work on my home for another year? Contracts had to be postponed until next year due to the Director's refusal to reconsider his action and/or grant a delay until after the summer. Everyone I talked to expressed their opinion that the punishment was too severe, too harsh, and not commensurate for a first-time offense, especially after 23 years of creditable, outstanding service to the government. The only conclusion I can make on why I was treated so harshly is the Director retaliated because I reported him for his alleged abuse of the EML orders and that I dared to question his promotion of a close friend whom I believe was not as qualified for the position. I understand the GAO required the Director to reimburse the government for the excessive EML trips his dependent took. The EEOC is presently looking into the promotion of his close friend.

I was in a state of shock from 25 May to 23 June (the day I received your brief which stated that in fact I did not break federal law, that I was not in violation of DoD policy, that, in fact, I was entitled to have anyone represent me). But until that date, I believed I had committed a great crime. I began to lose confidence in myself and in my work. I wondered what others thought about me. Job loss meant outstanding loans had to be re-negotiated and delayed. I began to lose my self-esteem. My wife and I were very low in spirit and health all summer. I had to carry my wife to bed several times because of the emotional strain. The possibility of losing my job and not being able to pay our mortgage on time were factors which caused this; however, I believe missing our son's graduation was very upsetting and made her ill. I lost over nine days due to sickness. Can the Director restore all this?

I thought I was a criminal for "flagrant violation of federal law" and thanks to the Superintendent, everyone else did, too. Not more than twenty minutes after the Superintendent gave me my propped letter of removal, he informed all the principals on island. For what purpose? When questioned about it, the Superintendent answered, "To stop rumors." I believe he wanted to create rumors as no one outside his office knew of this action with the exception of the Director and his staff.

I foolishly believed that the Director was sincere in wanting an explanation and a response to the proposed action. I foolishly believed that if I were honest and frank that the Director would reconsider and not take such severe action. I sincerely apologized and made a number of suggestions to resolve the situation; all to no avail. As a manager, I learned that discipline should not be punitive, especially on the first offense, but should be correctives and/or a warning given. I was not given this courtesy. These officials were not concerned with the propriety of the charges, but were out to remove me from this high school. I have been told that their minds were "set in concrete" and no matter what I said or did, nothing was going to change their minds.

In spite of your excellent briefs (four in all) and in spite of your brief which suggested DoDDS obtained legal counsel before they continue to violate the law by mischaracterization, they refused. Your briefs were very strong and still DoDDS refused to stop action against me. They were only concerned in getting me out and they knew the system favored them. They had nothing to lose but taxpayers money, so why not continue the action against me?

Every attempt by DoDDS was made to move me off this island. Orders were cut and a port call was made for me, although these were my responsibility. Even though DoDDS knew a stay was coming by the Special Counsel, an attempt was made by the CPO official to have me aboard an airplane 12 August. The Director ordered my principal to have my office packed out. The stay came at 0755 on 12 August. All of these attempts were to harass, disturb and to intimidate me into leaving.

The Director unleashed his fury after learning of the stay. He requested his financial staff to search out any improprieties in our tuition collection system, but as I understand it, backed off when he was advised the area office wasn't cleared to do so. Therefore, he directed his financial expert to audit our school financial books. The financial expert, who was a friend of mine, stated, "The Director is looking for something to hang you on, Dan, so if I were you, I would get out because he will never stop until he gets you out." Although the bookkeeper was in the States with the only set of keys and was due back in a few days, the Director couldn't wait and ordered the cabinets to be forced open (a crowbar was used) to get to the books. The auditors found a beautiful set of books with no irregularities. In fact, they recommended the entire Pacific Schools adopt the system used at Kubasaki. I had complete confidence they would not find any irregularities as Mrs. Shook, business teacher and our book keeper, was fastidious in her keeping of our financial records. The financial expert cautioned me again a few days before he left the island to "Get away because the Director won't rest until he gets you out."

The Director was searching for anything. He requested OSI to investigate my home leave because the CPO official "happened to read and remember an article, printed months ago, about a rather romantic comment made by a writer of a newspaper article that my wife and I visited France every summer." The Director tried to intimidate us by accusing us of fraud and abuse. I blew the whistle on the Director's fraud and abuse of the EML Program; therefore, he was trying to get back at me. They did not find any abuse.

Again, the Director got his logistical personnel to twist a cost-saving suggestion which I had made and which saved the government some $18,000 in such a way as to read that I actually cost the government some $24,000. Even though all of the top engineering staff at Kadena Air Base approved of my cost-saving idea, a person with no engineering background, the Director accused me of wasting the government's money. The point of the above items is that the Director was able to get his entire staff to say anything or to do anything against me. There was a concerted effort by the Director and some of his staff to find something against me. It was deliberate, intentional and unmerciful.

On the other hand, the Director was not interested in saving the government money. He had directed that I be assigned to an elementary position in mainland Japan. It would have cost the government over $9,000 to move me to Japan. I suggested, five

*times, to be assigned to Okinawa to one of 14 positions available.
The Director refused and insisted I would be most successful in
Japan. It would not have cost the government one penny to have
me remain on Okinawa. The Director's only concern was to get
me off this island, no matter what it would cost the government.*

*We started to dispose of items because we were informed our
weight allowance would be restricted. We gave away and sold
many items that we would have kept under normal conditions. We
still have items wrapped at this writing because we are not sure
what will happen.*

*My fellow colleagues have very little contact with me. People who
I thought were my friends stayed away. Some individuals I never
knew before came forward to help. I could tell you of some amusing
stories of administrators avoiding me in public places. Others have
sent word, saying how much they admire me and that they wish they
had the "guts" to stand up and be counted. I have the impression that
many administrators and even some staff people in the Director's
office support me with their thoughts. They are hoping I will be successful, but are afraid to support me openly because they "know how
the system works." Many are intimidated and are afraid. One thing,
you have very few friends in a situation like this. I wish I could
reveal the names of the persons who have helped and how they have
helped, but I must protect them for fear of retaliation by the Director.*

*The pressures from the Director's office would put us in a very
low mood and at times we were about to give up; then your briefs
would arrive and we would be up-lifted and given hope. We certainly had our highs and lows this summer. Four hours before we
were to get on the plane, the Special Counsel ordered a stay until
an investigation took place. There was an investigation and, as
you know, the report was very favorable to me. The Special Counsel does protect whistle blowers, and I am grateful.*

*The one high plus was my Supervisor. I was awarded a com-
mendable rating on my evaluation for school year 1981–82. This
was done even after the Principal heard of my removal. Pressure
was brought to bear on him, first by the Director, to change my*

rating "in the light of the proposed removal," and then by the other Director the next day. The Principal flatly refused to change my rating, stating, "Nobody tells me how to rate my people." The Director reminded the Principal that, "This will go to court and you will be right beside me." The Principal will pay the price for not going along. I will continue to pay the price as long as the Director is the supervisor. He has stated, "Dan will win the big one, but I will get him on a lot of little ones."

I want to prevent this from happening to others. I will do what I can to convince my representatives in Congress to change DoD and school policy as to not punish before there is an investigation, particularly in demotions or removals. A policy should exist wherein officials are held accountable for such actions. The Director, who knows how the system works, and knows that very little, if anything, can be done against him, hasn't spent a penny of his own money. I have spent nearly $6,000 of my own money. The Director had nothing to worry about as he had the resources of the United States Government and the taxpayers money. If he were held accountable for such drastic action, then he would have thought twice about being so unethical towards me. Believe me, I could never get away with punishing a student before there was an investigation, nor would you dare take such action against a teacher before there was an investigation. The Director can take such action against a teacher before there was an investigation. The Director can take such action against his administrators because we are not protected. No one will question or blow the whistle because they are afraid.

Herein lies the tragedy of this whole affair. We are in a profession where we try to train the mind to think, to respond, to question, to search out, to be inquisitive, to seek the truth—and yet when one applies these principles through a system which has been established by law to be used by federal employees, one is called "unfit" and "not a team player." I used the system I was entitled to and have a right, by law, to use (e.g., grievance, EEO and the Inspector General's Office).

If I have deliberately violated federal law, I am wrong and should be punished and suffer the consequences. Yet, after my superiors were told that they were stretching the law and were informed that their reading of these statutes were, charitably, characterized as absurd, they persisted in trying to destroy me. This I cannot forget. This should not have happened in America of all places, and with educators in particular, who are to set an example and who teach equal justice and opportunity for all. At this point I need to have my confidence restored in the system.

My father, God bless his soul, an Italian immigrant and a World War I American veteran, instilled a deep sense of patriotism in us for America and taught us to serve our country. As a civilian working with the military, I have that feeling of serving my country. I was rewarded with salary increases and outstanding award certificates. Now, after 24 years of serving my country, I've almost lost something in all this.

Someone has stated the light is still yellow for whistle blowers, but I say it is red.

Joe, please do what you can to have fair compensation for such needless suffering and please see if you can do anything so these officials will learn that they have an obligation and a responsibility to have a thorough investigation before taking such drastic action.

Sincerely,
Daniel A. DeCarlo
Box 693
FPO Seattle 98773

The proposed demotion and reassignment was still hanging over my head. Eric, while teaching at the University of Hawaii during this time, met a niece of Hawaii's Senator Daniel Inouye and explained my situation to her. With permission to use her name, Eric called the Senator in Washington who, in turn, contacted the Special Council's office and was able to stop the action against me until an investigation could be made. What a lucky break! Although I had an excellent attorney who worked hard on my case, it was the good senator who got the Special Council to come to Okinawa on my behalf. I owe so much to both Joseph Kolick and Senator Inouye.

A few weeks later the chief procurement officer, or CPO, for the Pacific School System visited me in my office at Kubasaki. Obviously, it was a friendly fishing expedition to determine my intentions following the investigations. In particular, he wanted to know whether I was considering a lawsuit. I said I had considered it, but I was not anxious to prolong my legal entanglements. If arrangements were made for me to be posted in Europe, I informed him, I'd forget about the whole horrible incident. Soon after, I received an offer to transfer to England as a GS-12, my current pay grade. I was advised by a local lawyer to hold out for a promotion to GS-13, but Genevieve and I, after discussing it, decided to end this crazy charade and take the transfer.

My new assignment took Genevieve and me to an Air Force base about fifty miles north of London, where I became principal at Chicksands Elementary and Junior High School. Upon my accepting the assignment, the personnel officer on Okinawa indicated that I was to leave within two weeks, although two months remained in the school year. They really wanted me to leave as quickly as possible after my "victory" in the hearings.

Although I didn't like the idea of leaving before the end of the school year at Kubasaki, my package included temporary duty assignment, or TDY, full household goods shipping, and concurrent travel if I left within two weeks. Several of my friends in the director's office advised me not to rush my move, as I had the department over a barrel, but I really didn't want to fight the system any more and decided to leave. Another friend, who worked in the CPO's office, warned me to get my income tax papers in order before we went to England. I thought this was strange advice, but as I always did my own taxes and knew everything that was claimed, I thought no more about it.

As we prepared to relocate, we said goodbye to teachers, neighbors, and the many Japanese friends we had made in our nearly fourteen years there, but nothing prepared us for the wonderful sendoff that teachers at my school and Genevieve's students at Ryukyu University gave us. When we arrived at the Naha airport and stepped out of the taxi, they greeted us with loud applause. We were overwhelmed with joy and sadness, laughter and tears. We left Okinawa with many fond memories.

We had been in England for four months when the American Embassy in London contacted me for an audit of my income taxes. This was the first time in my life this had ever happened! I wondered whether my friend's warning was merely coincidental or did he have inside information?

I contacted a former DoDDS colleague, also relocated to England, and asked if he could recommend a good tax advisor. He spoke highly of his own, so I scheduled a meeting. The advisor asked me to provide him with all my receipts and records to review in advance, and agreed to accompany me to the auditor's meeting at the London embassy.

The embassy auditor, who had been assigned the job of finding errors in my returns, was a very stern woman. In spite of her bulldog-like demeanor, she didn't have any clear points to make against me. When her faultfinding efforts briefly stalled, my taxman took the opportunity for which he had been waiting. In a calm, matter-of-fact way, he stated, "I have thoroughly reviewed my client's tax returns with the supporting documents and receipts and found that the government owes him a tax refund of nearly five thousand dollars." To my utter surprise, he had found thousands of dollars in allowable deductions I'd overlooked: travel and moving expenses, some of Eric's college tuition costs, medical expenses, and more. He hadn't mentioned one word of this to me, but, by golly, he was poised and ready to pounce. Instead of being raked across the coals, I was collecting a huge tax bonus from good ol' Uncle Sam. The auditing bulldog had to find another bone to chew.

I had strong suspicions that someone in the Pacific office had falsely reported me for cheating on my taxes. Four months later, the embassy in London again called to audit my current year's taxes. It was infuriating! I said, "I just had an audit and was cleared! Now, you go tell the person in the Pacific office who keeps reporting me that if he's going to do this, I will report him for all his mistresses and his affairs with subordinates... and I have names. I've kept records!" I knew this was blackmail, but I was angry. They never bothered me again.

As for the outstanding tax advisor, I retained his services for the next nine years, and he saved me money on many other occasions.

TEN

Embracing Europe

Chicksands AFB, formerly a British RAF base, where I was posted in England, was one of the most beautiful bases in Europe. The base was nestled in a lush, forested area. Chicksands Priory, a medieval monastery dating back to 1050, was the historic center-piece of the base. For over 500 years this strict religious facility housed devout monks and nuns, but in separate buildings to prevent contact between the men and women.

England is noted for its ghosts, and the most famous in the area was Rosetta, a young priory nun who broke her vow of chastity and became pregnant by a monk. For her crime she was forced to watch the public beheading of her lover and then sealed into a small space behind a ground-floor window. She wailed in anguish for days before she died. Her ghost is said to haunt the buildings and grounds, especially on the seventeenth, the day of her passing.

The priory's curator, Roger, invited me on a personal tour a few days after my arrival. He pointed out the false window on the left side of the main entrance and, behind the glass, the brick wall where Rosetta had been chained and left to die. For centuries to follow, sightings have been reported of a ghostly figure passing through walls, and turning some rooms so cold that no one could stay in them. One of the most popular stories tells of some ten American GIs who boldly attempted to stay overnight in the priory, camping out on the floor with heavy sleeping bags on the seventeenth of the month. During the night the room temperature suddenly dropped to an icy chill, and they gave up and fled.

Although priory personnel make it a point to leave the building before dark, Roger told me he once spent all night awake there on the seventeenth to photograph Rosetta's ghost. His efforts paid off: the resulting photo shows a sheer floating shape passing through a wall. The photo has been authenticated by a paranormal investigative committee at Oxford, which at that time had verified some 256 sightings of ghosts in England.

After touring the haunted priory and hearing the scary stories, I was still a non-believer. I headed for my office nearby and greeted my secretary, a no-nonsense Englishwoman who I'd only known since we arrived the previous week. "Hello, Pam," I said with a little chuckle in my voice. "I just toured the priory and heard those, ahem, ghost stories." Pam replied firmly, "Just you wait, Mr. DeCarlo! Rosetta will show up at our school before you know it, so be careful what you say. She plays tricks on people."

I soon found out what Pam was talking about. One of my responsibilities at Chicksands was to write a quarterly report for the superintendent for fifteen U.S. military dependent schools in England, and I had to be on my toes to meet the deadlines. Several weeks of work, as well as many evening hours, had already gone into my first report. With the cut-off date quickly coming up, I told Pam that I was going to leave the completed draft on top of my desk's outbox that evening and asked her to type it up first thing the next day.

When I got to work the next morning, Pam told me that she hadn't found my draft in my outbox or anywhere on my desk, so she assumed I'd taken it home to finish. But it should be here," I said, as I began to panic. "I put the report right here when I left last night!" Pam assured me, "Stay calm, we'll find it." Then she stopped and said, "Wait, this is the eighteenth! Rosetta was here last night." I think I was about to blow my top over this Rosetta superstition, but I tried to keep my cool. "Pam, I put it in my outbox," I said slowly and deliberately. "And now it's not there."

But I wasn't calm. I was frantic because there was no way I could recreate the report from memory and have it ready by its due date. We checked the closets, cupboards, file cabinets, wastebaskets, and the floor under the desks and tables. She was rummaging under the sink in my office when she called out, "I found it!" and pulled out the folder from among some old, dried-out potted plants. I was terribly relieved and completely baffled. "I knew we would find it," Pam told me. "You see, she's not a mean ghost, just a mischievous one. No harm done."

Pam's professionalism as a secretary was unsurpassed. Nothing ever ruffled her. As dear old friends, we have remained in contact over many years. I would not have believed this incident if it hadn't happened to me.

Chicksands Air Base was a large spy base, equipped with huge antennas for tracking Russian satellites and monitoring their communications. Technicians working in high-security underground facilities conducted secret snooping operations around the clock. Support personnel were located above ground. Six hundred students in kindergarten through the eighth grade attended the school.

I was school principal of Chicksands and very much enjoyed my work. The faculty worked well together, and we accomplished quite a lot in many different arenas, such as pushing to build a new gymnasium, reorganizing classrooms and storage areas to create space for art and music rooms, and implementing many worthwhile programs to benefit the students. In addition to our annual participation in the popular skiing program, Classe de Neige, we organized fairs, took field trips, held variety shows, and created outstanding programs for school assemblies.

I also wanted our school to be progressive — to offer students the opportunity to develop their computer skills — as we had at Kubasaki High in Okinawa. Although the base had neither teachers trained for computer classes nor the money set aside for such an endeavor, we managed to raise the funds on our own. Within two years, our fundraising efforts, consisting primarily of barbecues and community fairs, had generated $35,000 to build the first elementary school computer center in the DoDDS European area. area (I also built the first computer center in the pacific area at Kubasaki High School). Every student from kindergarten to eighth grade had a weekly computer session with volunteer tutors on one of thirty brand new Commodore Amiga machines, very state-of-the-art for 1985.

It was at Chicksands as school principal that I first had to fire a teacher. I had a two-inch thick file on the man, filled with complaints from students, parents, other teachers, his landlord, and his neighbors. Even the cafeteria workers in the PX had related how he often ate half his meal and then asked for his money back. Just for curiosity, I phoned the New York school where he'd been employed previously. "When we heard he was hired to work in Europe," they told me, "we were so glad to get rid of him." To further bolster my action, I looked at his hiring records and found that the U.S. interviewer had stated, "Don't hire this person." Somehow he had fallen through the cracks, and it was now up to me to do something about it. Considering the thousands of teachers involved in the overseas system, one renegade teacher is not bad. Still, when students, my number one priority, are involved, one bad teacher is one too many.

The teacher in question was a first year DoDDS employee. As I pointed out to him and the union representative when we met, he could be fired without cause or explanation within his first year per his contract. He did not protest, and he packed up and shipped out.

A most unusual experience I had was when our young cleaning lady came to my office and reported that she had found a pair of "messed up" shorts in the boy's rest room. We thought it unusual to find such an item, and since the shorts were size 44, I concluded that it had to be a large boy. I checked with the eight grade teacher regarding any unusual odors in the class room. None were detected. The next day the same thing occurred. Early in the morning, the same janitress complained about finding a pair of "messed up" shorts in the boys rest room. Again I investigated, but couldn't find a large boy that seemed to have a problem. On the third day, the same thing happened and this time the janitress threatened to resign. I had to do something.

I decided to visit the eight grade classes and visit each boy personally. I leaned over them, pretending to examine their work, and at the same time took a deep "sniff." I did this with each boy in the eighth grade classes but didn't find anyone that gave off a "distinctive aroma." I thought this was unusual, since it had to be a large boy. But I had to solve the problem or I would lose a cleaning person. I continued my search for the "smelly" boy with the seventh graders. Again, I paid a visit to each boy in those classes with the familiar, "Hi, how are you doing?" and at the same time, I took a deep breath. I struck out!

I refused to give up my search for the boy with a missing pair of shorts, so I decided to go to the sixth grades with the same routine. "Hello," sniff, and move on. Unfortunately, those students didn't produce an answer to the puzzle either. With the determination of a bloodhound (and blessed with an Italian nose), I pursued my prey. I went to the fifth grade teachers, my last hope of finding the culprit. As I looked over the group, however, I could see there was no way in the world any of them would wear a size 44 pair of shorts. Still I pressed on, visiting each boy with my cheerful, "Hello and how are you doing?" with my nostrils working overtime. I struck out again. "Impossible!" I thought. "Where did I go wrong? What did I miss?"

I was disappointed that I had so diligently searched for the culprit, yet failed. As I left the fifth grade and walked down the hallway, I passed the fourth grade classroom. "No," I decided, "I wasn't going to search any more." But then I reflected, "I've spent about two hours with no results. Why not finish the job?" So I entered the fourth grade class and spoke with the teacher. Nevertheless, I had little expectation of finding the owner of these very large pair of shorts.

I began my routine of sniffing and saying hello to each boy in the first row. At the fifth boy in the row, my nostrils flared at that familiar odor. Finally, I had "struck gold!" I asked the teacher if

I could speak with the student in my office and then escorted this good size, but not overly large, boy to my office. There he confided that he was having trouble and didn't know what to do. I called his father, who immediately came to my office. After hearing the story, his immediate reaction was, "I was wondering what was happening to my shorts!"

As we discovered, the boy had run out of his own shorts so he went to his father's room and selected something to wear. That explained the large size of the shorts found in the boy's restroom. Of course, looking for such a large boy had thrown us off the trail. It appeared that some meds the boy was taking were too strong, and he was too ashamed to tell anyone. I felt so sorry for the hapless lad. Of course, there was no way in the world that I would punish this little fourth grader, but I did come close to losing a hard-to-find janitress. Thus ended the "oversized shorts" caper.

Disciplining students was also part of the job. At Chicksands we had another "bathroom incident." A second grade teacher escorted one of her students into my office. She was very upset and asked me to reprimand him for apparently urinating on another boy in the restroom. After explaining the situation, she spun on her heels and left him standing sheepishly in front of my desk. Furrowing my brow, I seriously inquired, "So, what happened, Johnny?" "It was an accident, Mr. DeCarlo," he pleaded. "It was really an accident." With a doubtful look, I pointed out, "The toilet was in front of you and the boy was behind you. Now how can that be an accident?" He hesitated before shyly giving his side of the story. "Well, I heard a noise behind me and when I turned, my whole body followed," he explained. "And I wet my friend." I dutifully carried out the reprimand and dismissed Johnny back to the classroom. After closing the door to my office, I burst out laughing at the innocence and imagination of children.

***

Genevieve and I loved being at Chicksands. We were conveniently located near all there was to see and do in England: Stonehenge, Cambridge, Oxford, Stratford-on-Avon, and much more. Just the sights in London were enough to keep an interested visitor busy for years!

I kept busy with my school work and improving the facilities at the school. We had covered walkways built connecting the primary school with the middle school. We had a gymnasium constructed that included a stage, or in other words, a "gymtorium," where we had assemblies, music recitals, and talent shows. We had field trips, sporting activities, a horseback riding program, and we developed a music program. We also had a two week class in the French Alps, complete with ski lessons! There were school fairs, cookouts, and contests to support our computer lab and other activities. If the government didn't provide for us, we raised the money to do it ourselves. I called Chicksands "The best little school in USAFE."

I worked hard during the day but at night I used one of our empty classrooms for my hobby. As mentioned in an earlier chapter, I bought a train set for Eric when he was six years old. Over the years I bought accessories for the collection but I never had a room large enough to build the complete set. At Chicksands, after school each evening I returned to the vacant room and built the complete set with eight engines running at the same time. I had a master control board with switches, a roundhouse, and a turntable. I worked for a good two months and if I do say so myself, it was a masterpiece!

At different times I invited kindergarteners and the first three grades to see it in operation and run it themselves. To me, it was the greatest thrill to watch the reactions of those children and I hope I turned on the desire in some to have their own set someday. The adult visitors and parents were quite impressed, but frankly it was the children's reactions that I really enjoyed most. After that, I never again set up the complete set and eventually gave it to my nephew in Paris for his family.

Now in our fifties, we began to experience a few aging issues. Mine made itself felt one clear morning while driving to work. I had stopped at an intersection, looked both ways, and began to drive across when suddenly a bicyclist appeared, riding along from the crossing direction. If he hadn't quickly swerved, we would have collided. It was absolutely frightening and shook me to the core. I was most disturbed that I hadn't seen him when he was right there.

My eyesight had been gradually weakening for several years from macular degeneration, a genetic trait among the men in my family. It had already affected my older brother Tony, who eventually went blind. I realized at that moment that I would have to give up driving immediately. Arriving home that night, I handed my keys to Genevieve, saying, "This is it. I came very close to hitting a man on a bike today, so here are the keys. Please drive me to work from now on. I just don't have the peripheral vision to see to my right or left." And I never drove again.

Although Genevieve was doing well, her middle-aged bones were becoming fragile and her doctors advised her not to ride. She resigned herself to giving up her passion and turned to painting. Soon she was producing oils and watercolors, without ever having an art lesson! She was talented and accomplished in everything she did, so it came naturally.

Every summer we returned to France, taking the ferry across the English Channel. On one of our trips, we passed through a storm, a truly hair-raising experience. We feared for our lives as the boat lurched and leapt from side to front to back in the high winds and rough seas. Passengers were getting sick all over the place, and dishes and glasses in the restaurant came crashing out of their cupboards. Our faces were still green when we reached the port of Dunkirk and offloaded our car for the drive to France, about a day and a half away. Right then and there, we resolved to locate to the continent as soon as possible, but it would be several more years before we had the opportunity. We remained in England for nine wonderful years, from 1983 until 1991, when Chicksands base closed down and its personnel transferred.

With U.S. bases and their schools gradually closing throughout western Europe, there was an excess of administrators without assignments. To address this problem, DoDDS initiated a new program offering classroom positions to administrators at their same pay level for three years. After this time they would revert to a teacher's annual salary, a pay drop of $30,000. Well, our government is very generous: a buyout bonus of $25,000 was also included in the deal. I found the offer very intriguing. Although administrators earn more than teachers, they often work longer hours and have fewer holidays. Of the fifty who applied to this voluntary program, I was relieved to be among the twelve select-ed. I now had my administrator's salary but with teacher's hours and holidays. We regretted leaving the Chicksands school system, with its great facilities and outstanding faculty, but the offer from the government was too good!

During my thirty-eight years with the overseas school system I created personal scrapbooks of photos, articles, special occa-sions, cartoons, flyers, and events from the schools where I had worked since 1958, beginning at Paris American High School. Continuing this hobby at each school to which I had been as-signed, I had amassed thirty-eight thick scrapbooks in organized binders to include everything that had to do with our school system and each particular school. Before leaving England I donated the scrapbooks to the American Overseas School His-torical Society in Wichita, Kansas. I was told it was the largest known collection of scrapbooks for the overseas school system. I also donated some twenty high school yearbooks. Not only was this a very gratifying retirement project, but it also cleared some much-needed space in our apartment!

***

My new teaching assignment took us to Casteau, Belgium, the home for Supreme Headquarters Allied Powers Europe, or SHAPE. This NATO military installation had relocated from Paris in 1967 and was now well-established, twenty-four years later. The base elementary and high school student population consisted of up to nineteen nationalities speaking seventeen dif-ferent languages. Americans comprised half of the enrollment.

We rented a house from a Belgian family in the suburbs of Mons, and we couldn't have asked for better landlords. Carlos and his wife Mary Ann were hard workers who bought and fixed up old houses and rented them out. This gracious couple and their two daughters became our friends, introduced us to their friends and extended family, and took us on many trips around the gorgeous countryside. We toured ancient cathedrals, visited museums, and gazed in wonderment at the largest canal locks in the world.

Belgium was the locale of "Expo '58," the first major world's fair after World War II. Over thirty years later, a number of the original exhibits were still popular visitor attractions in Brussels. The Atomium, a gleaming, futuristic, multi-storied representation of a single atom accompanied by its protons and neutrons, served as the anchoring feature of the expo. Various countries contributed their own impressively large and architecturally advanced exhibits, blending together harmoniously in the massive area. In 1958 I had taken a side trip to visit the fair with a teaching buddy while working in Paris and courting Genevieve. I was happy to find the now historic grounds with its pretty park and quaint German restaurants still in good use. My favorite food in Belgium was the mussels with French fries, surely the best in the world!

Genevieve was always able to occupy herself while I was busy at the school. She enjoyed playing piano, preparing sumptuous meals in our home to entertain friends and family, visiting nearby museums and galleries, and tending the roses and herbs in our garden. Always willing to help out with extracurricular activities at school, she chaperoned dances and field trips. Genevieve's warm personality and gift for language and the arts made her welcome in any setting.

My fifth grade class at SHAPE American Elementary School had thirty students. I taught all subjects, including English, social studies, science, math, art, and history. This enthusiastic age group dived into the many projects we dreamed up together.

Students eagerly took on different responsibilities in the classroom. We had a "zookeeper" for maintaining our menagerie of rabbits, hamsters, guinea pigs, and the fish aquarium. Our "botanist" was in charge of plants, including colorful potted geraniums along the windowsills and the out-of-control sweet potato vine that was trying to take over the whole room. A different student took over these positions every month, so everyone had a turn. When the school president or other visitors toured the school, members of the class were ready to show their social skills, politely escorting guests around the room to explain various projects and introducing student officers who then explained their duties.

We initiated a student council for fourth through sixth grades, and coincidentally, most of the council's officers were in my class. The student council sponsored art shows, music programs, field trips, and a very successful annual variety show.

Every student was special in his or her own way. One of our artistically talented students agreed to paint holiday scenes in our room's large windows at Christmas time. The school provided the paint, and everyone loved the finished result.

We started a store, named "Cash and Carry," in our classroom to sell school supplies. We purchased the items at the PX and marked them up ten percent. I procured an old cash register for our use. Volunteers served as treasurer and store manager. When our store opened at noontime, students from other classes, excited to do their own shopping, lined up to buy pencils, scissors, and erasers. To raise money to purchase supplies, we issued stock certificates as an investment in the store. Students bought stock at a dollar per share with a maximum of four shares. When the business closed at the end of the year, the investors had doubled their money. The Dow Jones would be a major disappointment compared to these returns.

I also organized the music, chess, and computer clubs, the ski class, and field trips. On our trips to the space museum, we were thrilled to walk through the interior of the Space Shuttle and sit in the cockpit.

To decorate our classroom, students made paper mache models of the solar system, with the sun, planets, ping-pong ball moons, and the Space Shuttle, all floating on strings suspended from the ceiling. We also built a life-sized bear and a formidable dragon from paper mache.

The student body selected a shark as their very first school mascot. The design of a friendly-looking shark was a big hit, and the t-shirts with its image were purchased by hundreds of students. As one of our art projects, every student made their own little paper mache shark head to be mounted on wood backing. I enclosed a personal message to each individual in their shark's head, before the head was glued to the backing, predicting what each student would be doing in ten years. Of course, I predicted success for each and every one of them in their area of talent or interest. On the last day of school, I gave instructions not to open the shark's head until the year 2004, although I figured most of the students opened the head as soon as they got home.

I felt very productive. I received many performance awards, but the greatest reward was providing students a creative educational experience. I wanted nothing more than to continue teaching for a few more years before I retired, but higher ups in the system deemed otherwise, wanting me to once again assume an administrative position as assistant principal. I dutifully complied, but to my delight I was able to remain in the classroom part-time teaching social studies to fifth graders until retirement. I owe this to the parents of some of my students who wrote letters to SHAPE administration asking that I keep my teaching position for the benefit of their children. I was deeply grateful for their kind support.

***

Throughout this period, Genevieve and I spent summers at Le Quanty in France, hosting international students at our Center for Intercultural Exchange. The four-acre Le Quanty estate was magnificent, truly breathtaking. One of the most impressive features, which I haven't mentioned, was the huge wine cave. Its fortress-like stone block walls were a meter and a half thick. Built partly underground in cool deep soil, the temperature remained perfect for wine storage throughout the year, regardless of the season. One of the many good friends we entertained at dinner gatherings was a connoisseur who provided us with a fine collection of wines to grace our cave. When we entertained, Genevieve, a gifted cook, served exquisite meals on the four hundred-year old dining table. The spacious outdoor patio, where Dr. Gavel and his wife Jackie hosted Franco-American Night, accommodated groups of twenty people.

Escargots were so common in this farm country that I could have gathered hundreds of them every day, if we could have consumed such a quantity. I assigned myself the position of "professional escargot collector," creeping around the grounds with a flashlight at night like a burglar. I placed the live snails in a box with handfuls of fresh lettuce for them to eat and cleanse their systems of any toxic plant residues, making them tastier and safe to consume. All our neighbors cultivated wine grapes, and snails gobbled up the leaves, damaging crops. The farmers didn't want to use any poisons on their precious vines, so the best pest control was eating the pests, and we never grew tired of escargot's tender buttery taste. By popular demand, I typed up a copy of my "famous" easy-escargot recipe to share with students and friends for many years.

Genevieve and I had expected the property to come into our possession sooner rather than later, but surprisingly the old ladies, who were still living on the property per our agreement, lived another eighteen years. As we came to know the Marsac area better, we learned that people from this region had the longest life spans among the French population and we met neighbors who were over one hundred years old. I was a bit apprehensive that the ladies might outlive us! Their amazing longevity inspired a friend of ours to draw up a cartoon showing the two wrinkled women standing at my headstone, saying, "Poor Mr. DeCarlo—98 years old. He was so young."

By 1990, both sisters were deceased, and we set ourselves to the task of renovating their side of the house, another big job for us! It appeared very few changes had been made to their part of the manor since it was built, possibly in the mid-1300s. The earliest written records for the property dated back to 1530, when it was referred to as a "very old house." Again we had to install electricity, running water, and a heating system. For the next few summers we also cleared the musty attic of cobwebs, grime, and rats, then boarded it up. We tore down flimsy partitions and built new support walls. A collapsed chicken coop was leveled and replaced with a broad patio overlooking freshly planted vineyards. There was always something that had to be done.

After spending the next few summers hosting international students at our Center for Intercultural Exchange, it was with saddened hearts that we had to give up our dream of expansion. Finding domestic help for hire in this rural location was impossible, and it was too much work for the two of us to do all the housecleaning, laundering the linens, and managing upkeep for our home when it served as a hosting facility. We came to terms with this decision and felt ready to enjoy a relaxing lifestyle in our comfortable chateau.

Eric visited La Quanty during the summers, and it was always a delight to see him and catch up in person. After graduating from Florida Institute of Technology and earning his master's degree at Old Dominion in Virginia, he went to the University of Hawaii for his doctorate in chemistry. In an elevator at the university he met his future wife, Sharon, who worked in the oceanography department. Genevieve and I flew to Hawaii for their flower-filled wedding in 1987. In 1990 Eric and Sharon brought their baby girl to France and we met our adorable nine-month old granddaughter, Talisa, for the first time. We wanted to spend every moment with her, and it tugged at our hearts when her parents took her home, and so far away!

When Talisa was four years old, she stayed with Genevieve and me for the summer, while Eric and Sharon attended educational events elsewhere in France. Talisa adopted two ducklings and a fluffy rabbit. Everywhere she went, the animals were sure to follow. The ducks toddled along behind her, and she cuddled the bunny as a mother tenderly cradles her infant. We didn't tell her until fifteen years later that her pets were livestock that would become dinner the following year. Having been unforgettably traumatized as a child by Twee-Twee's demise, I did not want to upset her with reality until she was old enough to understand.

As summer drew to a close that year, Talisa returned to Hawaii and the house seemed to lose a part of itself. We busied ourselves preparing the property for the change of seasons and returned to Belgium for the start of another school year.

A few months later, Genevieve and I flew to Hawaii to spend the holidays with Eric, Sharon, and Talisa. Every minute of every day our granddaughter's loving and inquisitive nature was a joy to behold. The time went too fast. When we were to return to Belgium, Talisa draped us with flower leis and told her mother,

"I want to go with Grandma and Grandpa. I'll be back tomorrow." We all laughed, but then we had tears in our eyes as our flight crossed the Pacific. During our layover on the West Coast, I had time to think. I took Genevieve's hand in mine, looked into her eyes, and spoke from my heart, "Life is short, my dear. I should retire soon, and we can spend half the year in Hawaii." Genevieve smiled in her gentle way and wholeheartedly agreed.

In the late summer of 1995 we put Le Quanty on the market. In addition to all the improvements we had made, we included the furnishings that were part of the property when we bought it nearly twenty-five years earlier. This included the ancient solid wood dining table, and several armoires dating from the fifteenth century. Moving from a seventeen-room French manor to a two-bedroom apartment in Honolulu meant paring down our possessions to a bare minimum. Cherished items with which we could not part were the hunter green sofa we had bought together in France in 1961, an elegantly-simple Danish Modern dining set with buffet, and a cedar-lined China cabinet. We also kept Genevieve's 300-year old Louis XIV chair, a family heirloom.

Pauvre Monsieur De Carlo!
98 ans   Il était si jeune!
(Poor Mr. De Carlo - 98 years old. He was so young)

The cartoon showing Le Quanty's previous owners as having outlived me

In 1996 we received an acceptable offer on Le Quanty. Since our expenditures on improvements had been substantial, we didn't make any money. Still, we were pleased that the new owners wanted to keep the home's original historic furnishings. Thus closed a satisfying twenty-five-year chapter of our lives, which we had enjoyed and shared with dear friends and family.

ELEVEN

Saying Aloha and Farewell

DoDDS did not have a mandatory retirement age. I would have been happy to remain in the system with SHAPE for many years to come, but both Genevieve and I wanted to be more involved with our granddaughter as she grew up. Upon returning to Belgium after our holiday trip to Hawaii, the DoD announced that it was offering an early retirement buyout of $25,000. What timing! If we were unsure about my decision to retire, it was banished from our thoughts. I applied and was granted retirement at the completion of that school year in the summer of 1994, which was my third year at SHAPE.

The next few months were a blur of activity, as I wound down my long and productive career. As both a teacher and administrator, there was much to do to close the school for the summer. I was also responsible for distributing the year's final report cards and other duties, while Genevieve was busy at home. Not yet having sold Le Quanty, we planned to spend three to five months in France and the rest of the year in Hawaii, so she had to allocate our belongings for separate shipments. We looked forward to spending half the year being grandparents to our little Talisa!

Our moves went smoothly. From Belgium, a substantial amount of our household goods were shipped at no cost to Hawaii, where it was placed in free military storage. The rest of our items were trucked to France. Everything arrived in excellent condition. What a government we have! After taxes, I received $17,000 of my $25,000 DoD retirement buyout, just what we needed to clear our mortgage on Le Quanty.

Eric and Sharon had bought a lovely home in lush Manoa Valley, convenient to their jobs at the University of Hawaii. Since becoming a family, they had outgrown Eric's two-bedroom apartment in nearby Kaimuki, so we bought the place. We made some renovations and settled in, enjoying winter in Hawaii, which is really only a concept. We filled our days creating fun activities with Talisa. We took her to the zoo and aquarium, swam at the beach, assembled puzzles, sang songs, read books, painted with watercolors, played with the train set, had picnics, went to her soccer games, and attended concerts in the park. Talisa loved Genevieve's cooking, understandably! They baked cakes and tasty treats together. Often, we took her to school and picked her up to have dinner with us. When Talisa slept over on her little rollaway next to Genevieve's side of our bed, she would hold her grandma's hand till she fell asleep. Everyone adored her. Even at a very young age she had sensible and witty things to say.

Talisa, who had turned five years old, joined us for a month when we went to Le Quanty that summer. When she returned to her parents, we realized that it was more important for us to be in her life full time than to remain in France, so we put Le Quanty on the market. In addition to our profound affection for our granddaughter, there were several reasons for this. The property continued to require much work. Also, Genevieve said the long trips were very tiring for her. We both knew this was best for us. The proceeds from Le Quanty, which, as noted previously, we sold in 1996, paid off our mortgage on our Hawaii apartment. We could now enjoy an unencumbered retirement without financial worries.

We adjusted to being in Hawaii full-time quite easily, as we'd spent the previous winter and several holiday seasons in Honolulu. The benefit of retirement is free time, yet I greatly missed being in the classroom. Remaining involved with energetic young people and their ever curious, developing minds was a source of great joy for me, so I began a second career as a substitute teacher at nearby elementary and high schools.

My government pension was adequate for a comfortable retirement, so I decided to give back my substitute teaching salary to the students in the form of annual scholarship awards. I wanted to encourage young people to further their education and pursue noble goals. For the first few years, I contributed to college scholarship funds for top students. Once I realized that these students received generous scholarships from foundations and corporations, amounting to as much as $50,000 dollars per student, I didn't feel that a portion of my modest proceeds would make a big difference in their academic goals. As they were already receiving plenty of encouragement to reach their objectives, I switched gears. I recognized that special needs students, labeled as "marginal," were the ones who most needed a boost toward some form of higher education. Many of these kids had an extraordinary quality: the courage to show up at school every day and do their best, knowing they would never become valedictorian. I worked with the schools to form programs for these students, and the administrators were wonderfully supportive. I estimate that I donated over $60,000 to Kaimuki High School alone from my twenty-three years of substituting there. I also substituted regularly at Aliiolani Elementary and Kaimuki Middle School and gave awards at these schools, as well.

Our time at home with family and my work at the schools kept us active and involved. Talisa developed an interest in playing the keyboard as a toddler and was now performing at recitals that her piano teacher had organized for her students. When she was thirteen years old, we took her to her first school dance. We cherished every moment of her growing years, knowing the time was flying by too fast.

In her junior year of high school, Talisa developed a serious eye infection from wearing contact lenses. An ulcer had formed very close to the pupil, and she risked losing her sight in that eye. Antibiotic eye drops had to be applied every two hours, day and night, and it was a precarious situation. The pain she suffered was almost unbearable, but the doctor saved her eye. Knowing how fortunate she was, Talisa declared, "I want to become an eye doctor, to help save people's eyes."

Genevieve continued with her Japanese language studies, although she was already skilled in reading, writing, and speaking. A perfectionist, she strived for constant improvement. Although she couldn't chance resuming her horse jumping, she found a stable on the other side of the island where she could be around horses again and do some dressage riding.

Genevieve also loved to travel. After living in Europe and Asia, she wanted to see America. We booked a Caravan Tours "Canyonlands" package and delighted in the superb highlights of the western states, including the spectacular Grand Canyon, majestic Rocky Mountains, spired temples of Salt Lake City, stately rock formations of Zion and Bryce national parks, and breathtaking Yellowstone. Along the way the temple spires of Salt Lake City inspired us. Our Snake River adventure was an exhilarating ride down churning rapids in an inflatable boat piloted by skilled steersmen, leaving us wobbly-kneed for several days.

On our Tahiti trip in the following year, we took ground tours to sparkling beaches and picturesque grass-shacked villages, and ferry boats to the more isolated scenic outer islands. Like young honeymooners, we held hands as we traveled and visited the sights. The highlight of this trip was seeing our old friends from Marsac, a French village near Le Quanty. We visited with Damian, his vivacious wife Isabelle, and their first two children. We'd known Damian since his childhood, when he determined at an early age that he'd be in the restaurant business. Working as headwaiter in a Tahiti hotel's exclusive eatery was a valuable steppingstone in his career. After leaving Tahiti the couple returned to France to settle on Ile d'Oléron, a small island off the Atlantic coast, where they opened a first-class restaurant and had three more fresh-faced children. What a pleasure it was to see

Damian marry a wonderful woman, happily pursue his dreams, and achieve great success.

The Pacific Northwest was next on our list. In Seattle we lunched at the top of the Space Needle, toured the enormous Boeing aircraft plant, shopped at colorful flower markets, dined on fresh seafood at the wharfs, and took boat rides on the river as snow-capped Mt. Rainier towered majestically in the distance.

Another memorable trip included Nevada, Utah, Arizona, New Mexico, and Texas. In Nevada we were amazed at the Petrified Forest, a rare geological phenomenon. In New Mexico, we climbed huge sand dunes that overlooked the historic 1940s White Sands atomic bomb test site near Alamogordo. In the incredible explosion, sand from the surrounding area melted to glass and probably remains radioactive to this day.

After our departure in 1983, Genevieve had remained in contact with many of her French language students in Japan. In 2005 we scheduled a return to Okinawa, advising her former students of our plans. When we arrived at Naha Airport and disembarked from the flight, a large "welcome" sign and a musical band in the airport lobby greeted us, much to our surprise! Genevieve's students adored and respected her as their sensei. For our entire stay, they did not allow us to spend our own money, no matter how I tried to convince them otherwise. At their polite insistence, they took care of our hotel bill, meals at restaurants, and gasoline costs. On our Guam stopover I had to exchange all the yen I had bought on the way over, because we hadn't used any! To express our gratitude for the wonderful trip, we sent gifts and letters.

***

At seventy-six-years old, Genevieve and I were unusually healthy senior citizens, which we attributed to our wholesome diet and active lifestyle. Neither of us needed any prescription medications. Looking forward to our next adventure, we began preparing for a trip to see the giant redwoods of Sequoia

National Park and Kings Canyon. Unexpectedly, however, Genevieve said she felt weak and listless.

After canceling our travel plans to California we began our long march to numerous doctors, MRI facilities, and medical labs to find the cause and hopefully a cure for Genevieve's listlessness, weakness, and around-the-clock fatigue. Test after exhaustive test, we searched for answers. Over the next several years we sought help from thirty-six doctors, most of whom were specialists, without ever reaching a diagnosis.Looking outside Hawaii, I contacted a specialist at a Mayo Clinic in California. After reviewing Genevieve's medical records, he phoned back several weeks later with discouraging news: "It would be necessary for you both to fly over here and spend a few days doing tests and scans, but after thoroughly reading her records I'd advise that you save your money. We can't help her. I'm very sorry, but there's nothing I can do for you." Still, I did not give up hope.

Genevieve fell out of bed one night, perhaps trying to get up for the bathroom, and injured her arm. I found a place for her at Maunalani Nursing Home for a month of rehabilitation. Genevieve had good care at Maunalani and was visibly improving. During my daily visits, the staff and I delighted in her sense of humor and sharp wit. Here are some of her most memorable comments that helped me get through this difficult period:

- When Genevieve was in bed recovering from her arm injury, a nurse was changing her Depends and told me I should learn how to change diapers. Genevieve quickly added, "Yes, he needs to learn for our next baby."
- As we watched nurses coming and going down a busy hallway, I said, "Boy, a lot of the nurses are pregnant here!" She nodded wisely, "The doctors have been busy."
- As she approached me using her walker, I smiled encouragingly, putting my thumb out to hitch a ride. "Sorry, no room," she said, breezing past me.

- One of the directors asked Genevieve why she wanted to go home. She replied, "I need to go home because a man can't take care of a house."
- In the dining room, a waiter asked what she'd like to drink. "You name it, we've got it: orange juice, cranberry, beer, wine," he recited. "I'll take gin!" Genevieve replied mischievously. The waiter was stumped, but I laughed because Genevieve never really drank.
- After we attended a meeting with Eric and the staff to discuss her progress, I told her I was very proud of Eric, how smart he is and how well he handles problems. Without a word she pointed to her head and nodded. Then she pointed to herself and smiled.

It always amazed me that my wife never complained. I can only attribute this to superhuman self-restraint. Through all the recent challenges and difficulties brought on by her declining health and from the past grief I'd caused with my job situations in Libya and Okinawa, she kept sight of the bright side, always believing things would get better. Her stabilizing influence and positive outlook helped me find my way out of some tough times.

After Genevieve returned home from Maunalani, I brought in a physical therapist to help her better use her walker, stabilize her balance, and maintain the progress she had gained. But physical therapy didn't reverse her condition, and it became risky for her to use the walker when we went out for groceries and such. There was no other option than to get a wheelchair. We continued going out, with me pushing her along as we conversed.

I hired Mary, a skilled and gentle caregiver, to assist with Genevieve's bathing and personal care during the day. In the evenings, I alone took care of her, helping her in and out of bed. She tried valiantly, but couldn't walk, or even stand, on her own. When I began to have back pain, I realized we could no longer manage her care in our small apartment. After a long search for a nursing facility to which we could relocate, I found a comfortable two-bedroom apartment on the fourteenth floor at One Kalakaua Senior Living, or OKSL. OKSL serves as a high-rise community for many active seniors, and we enjoyed a social life of bingo games, chair-exercise classes, dances, piano performances, a country fair, and a bake-off, which I won with my famous banana cream pie recipe! Genevieve also received the full-time care she needed and deserved. At the push of a button, a facility nurse or caregiver would be at the door ready to assist us at any hour. Upon relocating to OKSL, a burden of worry lifted off my shoulders and I felt lighter.

Mary continued to assist us, making sure that Genevieve got outside to fight off the boredom. Thanks to an energetic, green-thumbed resident and a good staff of gardeners, the grounds at One Kalakaua bloomed in a rainbow of flowers and fragrant herbs. It was the perfect place to get fresh air and sunshine, and they went daily. Mary pushed Genevieve along in her wheelchair to take in the sights, window-shop at Ala Moana, and feed birds in the park. Mary also helped ensure that she was well groomed and dressed in pretty outfits. Everyone complimented Genevieve for her natural beauty and youthfulness, and I proudly agreed with them.

Genevieve also had a speech therapist, who instructed her in daily exercises for enunciation. Genevieve's voice had become so soft and weak that it was barely audible. The therapist suggested that Genevieve might have a touch of Alzheimer's, causing her to hesitate and search her memory for words.

Genevieve received regular home visits from Jennifer, an excellent massage therapist well versed in the fragility of older people. Our doctor appointments continued, as well. She was now using a number of medications, but none made any difference. Genevieve's feet and ankles had become so puffy, possibly from sitting so much, that she couldn't wear her shoes anymore. To tone her legs and increase circulation, she used a pedal-exerciser while seated. This was a tediously boring exercise for a former champion equestrian.

Knowing, however, that it made me happy, she methodically turned the pedals. In the evenings we watched television together, holding hands in our side-by-side chairs. I don't know how many times we saw our favorite movie, the gorgeously entertaining *Phantom of the Opera*.

When asked, Genevieve always indicated that she was not in pain, but her muscle atrophy progressed at a worrisome rate. Searching for ways for her to regain her strength, we began swim therapy at a rehabilitation center. She seemed to enjoy it, which made the activity worthwhile. It involved transferring her safely in and out of the car, folding and loading the wheelchair, placing her on the poolside lift to be slowly lowered into the water, and a sit-down shower and change of clothes afterwards. The swim therapist, James, was wonderful with Genevieve. He helped her relax as the water supported her weight, and she trusted him completely. In the water she had no fear of falling and she responded well to his soothing encouragement. I went into the pool also, staying by her side. Perhaps having me there made it seem more like floating around in a pool than having therapy, but the fact is I didn't want to be away from her.

In just a few months, Genevieve lost her ability to speak. Extreme stiffness in her neck, an apparent result of her illness, even made it hard for her to nod her head to answer questions. For such a skilled communicator, this must have felt incredibly isolating. To communicate her likes, dislikes, and moments of frustration, she used facial and hand expressions. Her frustration showed when she was no longer able to manage simple tasks on her own, such as brushing her teeth, and it was heart-wrenching to see her face reflecting these emotions.

Eric and Sharon joined us weekly in the OKSL dining room for a family dinner, and Genevieve's eyes sparkled when Eric spoke to her in his perfect French. Talisa, who had started her first year of college out of state, came to see us whenever she was in town. Together with a dozen friends, we celebrated Genevieve's eightieth birthday with champagne, balloons, and funny hats. Genevieve glowed in a glittery paper crown, and we called her "Queen Genevieve."

Looking for more activities, I discovered a therapeutic riding facility on the other side of the island that was happy to work with us. A caregiver drove us to the facility, and Genevieve and I enjoyed the scenic route along the south shore's turquoise beaches and grassy hillsides. When we arrived, strong, capable hands transferred Genevieve from a wheelchair-lift platform to the back of a docile horse. Genevieve smiled tentatively at me from under her safety helmet while she was led slowly around a shady arena. On the way home we stopped to leisurely slurp a soft-serve ice cream cone at the Waimanalo McDonald's, known locally as the slowest fast-food stop in the entire franchise.

The OKSL nurses checked residents' vitals as often as needed. During one such visit, the nurse checking Genevieve's blood pressure noted that it was dangerously low and advised us to take her to the hospital. Knowing my wife's preferences, I decided to take the city bus rather than a noisy, traumatizing ambulance. Along with her caregiver, we boarded the bus to Straub Hospital and arrived at the emergency room in a matter of minutes. Determining that Genevieve needed a boost of fluids and nutrition, they admitted her to a room for twenty-four hours. The reason for her dehydration was apparently her difficulty swallowing, perhaps a symptom of dementia. Although we had been vigilant giving Genevieve ample water and juice, she sometimes just held the liquid in her mouth.

This hospital stay was not without a mishap. It's not clear what happened, but when I checked on her in the hospital room, her feeding tube had been pulled out and was spilling all over her and the bed. Once they reconnected the fluids, Genevieve was soon stabilized enough to return home. Upon her release, a nurse suggested that we buy toddler-style drinking cups with sipper-straws. This improved the situation somewhat.

One of Genevieve's helpers, a woman with knowledge of nutrition and natural remedies, noticed that Genevieve had a darker-colored outline around the irises of her eyes, indicating exposure to certain toxins. She asked if Genevieve had consumed a great deal of fish in her life, including fish from rivers, or if she had frequently swum in canals or streams. I said, as far as I knew, her eyes always had the color variation, but she probably did swim in streams as a child and fish was one of her favorite foods. I couldn't think of any toxins Genevieve might have been exposed to in her life, but it was suggested that we try something called "intravenous chelation," which draws metal toxicity out of the bloodstream. I was willing to try anything once, if it would help my Genevieve get well again. We scheduled an appointment with a special clinic downtown, although the therapy was very expensive. After one treatment, surprisingly, the swelling in Genevieve's feet and ankles diminished quite obviously, and her shoes fit comfortably again. But if it only helped her feet, it wasn't worth continuing the treatments.

I wanted to make special plans for our upcoming fiftieth anniversary on December 19, a few months away. Hoping Genevieve would be able to take a short, easy trip, I inquired with a travel agency about the popular seven-day, inter-island cruise around Hawaii. I wasn't concerned about the cost, but rather her comfort and safety. Mary had already agreed to join us as full time caregiver, but the decision to take the trip or not had me pacing the floor. Eric was hesitant as well, logically pointing out that his mother didn't seem strong enough for travel. Thinking aloud to Genevieve's other caregiver, I asked, "What would you do in my situation?" She looked back at me, speechless for a moment. Then she chose her words carefully. "If... if you didn't have her here with you... next year, would you wish you had taken the cruise now?" I picked up the phone and dialed the travel agent.

Due to her difficulty swallowing, Genevieve had recently lost weight. I was quite concerned knowing that she needed the nutrients to sustain her, now more than ever. We were scheduled to leave in the third week of October, a month away. Although it was hard to know how much she understood, I still spoke to her as if nothing had changed. "Darling, we're taking a cruise," I told her excitedly, "for our fiftieth anniversary!" I felt even more gleeful when her eyes sparkled with silent acknowledgement. Suddenly her appetite returned, with a hunger I'd never seen in her before! For the next four weeks she ate everything put in front of her. If she couldn't hold a utensil, she used her hands. We offered to assist, but she flatly refused, eating with the speed and enthusiasm of someone who'd just been rescued from a desert island. Her face showed purpose and determination as she ate. She gained at least ten pounds prior to the trip, and some of her clothes were too tight! Her caregivers noticed the difference, too, when lifting her.

Genevieve's face and figure filled out, her eyes were bright and alert, and she looked much healthier just in time for the cruise. I felt encouraged and relieved. The cruise was perfect, and we had a fantastic time! At every opportunity the boat staff and passengers congratulated us on our fifty years together. Attentive to my wife's every need, Mary kept her safe and comfortable, never leaving her side, and Genevieve's demeanor was perky and happy. I didn't notice it at first, perhaps due to the constant activity onboard, but Genevieve wasn't eating much at all.

* * *

As soon we got back, Genevieve began losing weight. Eating and drinking required extreme effort. Years ago we had thoroughly discussed our advance directives, and we had both signed the documents confirming our wishes to not be kept alive by tube feeding, oxygen, or any emergency measures or artificial means. So I pleaded with her to swallow food and liquids.

I consulted with a hospice nurse. She explained how some people with dementia or other illnesses can lose their ability to swallow, at which point the family makes a decision on behalf of their loved one. The nurse told us that based on her experience, Genevieve might only last a week or two under

these circumstances. Since Genevieve had made her preferences clear at a time when she was of sound mind and body, I
understood my obligation to respect her wishes. But it tore at
my heart.

Per my request, a priest came to see Genevieve and pray
with us. Thanking the Father sincerely for his words of kindness, I walked with him to the elevator. Returning to our door,
I thought about Christian teachings: how our belief in God, a
lifetime of faith, and our good deeds will bless us into Heaven.
Such reassurance should have been comforting, but I wanted my
Genevieve here with me all my life, to have and to hold, and to
smile at me in her loving way.

I would have given anything to keep Genevieve alive and vi-
tal. Medical science had failed us. No doctor, medicine, hospital,
exercise, therapy, or prayers had brought the miracle I wanted now. I couldn't accept that she was slipping away. We were
supposed to grow old together and take care of each other for
many more years. "It's not fair," my mind repeated constantly. "It
shouldn't happen this way! I'm still walking around in reasonable health while she has only days to live. It's just not possible.
It's not right."

I knew her life was being cut short by reasons unknown, and I
needed to have hope for something, anything. In mid-November of
2009, I hoped she would live until our anniversary on December
19, for me to tell her again how much I loved her, for what an honor
and privilege it was to have her as my wife for fifty years.

Genevieve received excellent care at OKSL's in-house hospice
facility, where there were private rooms for family members to
spend time with their dear ones and prepare themselves for loss.
The wonderfully sympathetic hospice nurses stopped in regularly
to answer our questions and check on her comfort. I sat by Genevieve's bedside every day, holding her hand, touching her soft hair,
and talking to her. When awake, she often had a faraway look to
somewhere beyond the ceiling, and her breathing was labored but
rhythmic. At my request, her caregivers kept her company. I didn't

want her to be alone when I couldn't be there. As Genevieve rested, I sometimes whispered to the nurses, not knowing if she could hear or understand, inquiring about Genevieve's remaining time.

One day an attendant came in to freshen up the room. To straighten the bedding, it was necessary for her to momentarily lift Genevieve up from the bed. Then the unthinkable happened. She took a wrong step, lost her balance, and dropped Genevieve in a barely controlled, backwards movement onto the bed with a thump. Genevieve, who had lately been rather weak and un-responsive, reacted to this unexpectedly poor treatment with a wide-eyed look of horrified disappointment. We all saw the look, plain as day. The embarrassed attendant gave a clumsy apology. I glanced at Genevieve's surprised caregiver who looked back at me, and we both knew the same thing at the same moment: Genevieve still knew very well who she was, where she was, and what was going on around her. And she needed to be treated with respect and dignity, even if she was dying.

I checked on Genevieve at every opportunity. On my visits I kissed her warm, rosy cheek and told her I loved her. Sometimes she was resting, but I believed she knew I was there by her side. One day I stopped in for a short visit, telling her I'd be back very shortly. Surprisingly, she looked at me and summoned up the strength for a tiny smile. I smiled back and told her I loved her. Elated at what just happened, I headed upstairs to our apartment.

While I was out of her room, Eric stopped by for an impromptu visit to see his mother. If I had known his plans, I would have stayed to see him. Entering her room, he noticed that his mother's breathing required audible effort, her upper body rising and falling as her lungs struggled to fill with air. He nodded to the caregiver sitting quietly in a far corner of the room, who asked, "Do you want to be alone with your mom?" Eric shook his head, "You can stay. I was on my way to a conference and detoured, thinking this would be a good chance to see her." Ever the scientist, Eric has never been a believer in metaphysical forces. He pulled a chair close to her, touched her forehead and hair, and said with great tenderness,

"C'est Eric. Je t'aime, Mamma." A moment later, she gave several loud gasps, exhaled, and stopped, eyes still looking upward. Eric looked questioningly at the caregiver, who whispered, "She did this once before for a minute." He waited, resting his arm lightly on his mother's and watching her face for an eternity of two or three minutes, but he already knew she was gone. Eric kissed her cheek one last time and softly drew her eyes closed, then walked with heavy steps to find me.

I had left the apartment and started down the hall when Eric stepped out of the elevator, his eyes telling me what I didn't want to believe. "Mamma est morte," he said. He held my arm to support me as I broke down and cried, "I was just there! I was coming right back! I should have been there to say goodbye," I sobbed. "I should have been there for her." Eric's words were comforting. He said she went peacefully, and then he offered to escort me back to her bedside. I couldn't go back. I wanted to remember the sweet smile on her beautiful face and in her eyes, as I last saw her. I will cherish her forever.

***

On December 2, 2009, a few weeks before our fiftieth wedding anniversary, my beloved wife slipped away. I was numb with disbelief and didn't have any idea how I could go on without her. She was so much a part of me. I couldn't fathom being alone. To avoid agonizing over the uncertainty of the future, I kept myself busy handling her final arrangements and the necessary legal matters.

After receiving her ashes from the funeral home, I placed them in a covered Lauhala basket and decided to scatter them at sea. Eric suggested a lovely spot at Diamond Head Beach where he often surfed. So, on a gorgeous Hawaiian day in late December, our small group of a dozen family and friends met at the top of the pathway leading to the beach. My family draped me with flower leis. Talisa held my hand, and in the other I carried Genevieve's remains in the flower-bedecked basket. Together we all walked quietly down the slope to the sand. Eric placed the basket on

his surfboard, and with Talisa on her board they paddled out together. The rest of us sat on the sand, watching them scatter the
ashes and flowers among the waves.

GENEVIEVE CERBOS DECARLO

AUGUST 17, 1929—December 2, 2009

Genevieve is survived by her husband Daniel, her son Eric, her granddaughter Talisa; and three sisters, Madeline Jacquinet, Andrea Cerbos, Susan Mullins; and brother, Jean Cerbos.

A Service of Remembrance

Celebrating the Life of Genevieve Cerbos DeCarlo
March 6, 2010
One Kalakaua Senior Living
Honolulu, Hawaii

WELCOME. . . . . Daniel De Carlo

INVOCATION. . . . . Father Tim Eden

MEDITATION. . . . . Father Tim Eden

EULOGY . . . . Dr. Eric De Carlo

INTRODUCTION OF GUESTS . . . . . Daniel De Carlo

O GENEVIEVE, SWEET GENEVIEVE
by George Cooper

O Genevieve, I'd give the world
To live again the lovely past!
The rose of youth was dew-impearl'd,
But now it withers in the blast.

I see thy face in every dream,
My waking thoughts are full of thee,
Thy glance is in the starry beam
That falls along the summer sea!

Fair Genevieve, my early love!
The years but make thee dearer far.
My heart shall never, never rove;
Thou art my only guiding star.

For me the past has no regret.
What ever the years may bring to me
I bless the hour when first met,
The hour that gave me love and thee.

CHORUS

O Genevieve, sweet Genevieve,
The days may come, the days may go,
But still the hands of memory weave
The blissful dreams of long ago.

IT BROKE OUR HEARTS

It broke our hearts to lose you,
you did not go alone.
For part of us went with you,
The day God called you home.
You left us beautiful memories,
Your love is still our guide,
And though we cannot see you,
You are always by our side.
Our family chain is broken.
And nothing seems the same,
But as God calls us one by one,
The chain will link again.

THALYA'S EULOGY TO GENEVIEVE

At the memorial service for my dear Genevieve, Thalya, one of her caregivers, gave the following eulogy:

There was a popular film in the theatres last year which told a man's life story backwards, beginning with him as a senior citizen and ending at the time of his birth. This reminds me of how I got to know Genevieve. I came along in the last months of her life, as a helper and caregiver.

At first I knew little about her and I had many questions in my mind. I knew that she was the mother of my friend, Eric, mother-in-law to Eric's wife, Sharon, and grandmother to Talisa. I was very interested in learning about Genevieve's life and experiences, but these were yet for me to discover, as her life story unfolded gradually over the coming months.

Already impaired in her speech and mobility by the mysterious ailment which eventually claimed her, she was still able to communicate with her facial expressions and body language. This helped me to understand her needs and help with her care. Every day, more about her character, talents, and accomplishments were revealed to me without any need for her to speak of them.

On rainy days, when we couldn't go outside for fresh air, she liked to play card games or board games such as Chinese Checkers, Dominoes, or Spill 'n Spell. Dan gave me fair warning that Genevieve had superhuman determination, always excelled in her endeavors, and was highly competitive. I soon found that out for myself.

Her love of horses and horsemanship was our common thread. I found that she was captivated when I told her of all the horses I had known, from their magnificence to their mischief. She was spellbound when listening to my equine experiences so I kept telling her those tales until I ran out of horses to tell stories about.

As the weeks passed by, Genevieve and I spent many of our days together. I learned—sometimes by trial and error—of her personality, her preferences, her favorite foods (summed up as fish and chocolate), the elegant clothes which defined her style, and her refined manner.

I enjoyed bringing out the numerous photo albums and loose pictures of the many travels and adventures that Dan and Genevieve had collected in their 50 years together. I asked her about the people and places in the photos and through the stories they told, along with Dan's anecdotes and my daily interactions with Genevieve, I began to understand her life story.

When viewing photos of Genevieve in her youth, I asked her to tell me about her hometown, her maiden name and its origins, and her family and siblings. I wrote down the places and names from her childhood. I wanted to gain insight about her early life and the influences that had formed her. Genevieve never lost sight of who she was and what was important to her.

Although I knew Genevieve only in the last year of her life, she added profound value to my life experience. I am very grateful to have known her. Genevieve was blessed with many natural talents and abilities but I believe her greatest blessing was her family, and Dan, for his love and devotion and the lifetime they have shared together.

TWELVE

Starting over Alone

Genevieve's former students in Japan had heard about her passing, and I received their outpouring of sympathy in dozens of cards and letters, expressing their great respect and love for their teacher. In early March of 2010, I held a "celebration of life" dinner in memory of Genevieve in the multi-purpose room at OKSL. I compiled my favorite photos of her and pasted them on large poster boards to highlight the many joyful times we shared. Dear friends and family told stories, read eulogies, and said kind words in her honor.

With Genevieve's passing, I was now alone in the apartment. I knew Genevieve wanted me to continue on with life, to enjoy our family, to see our granddaughter finish college and start her profession and, perhaps, to know our great-grandchildren some day. Without her presence, however, I didn't feel right about being there or anywhere, for that matter. When our former apartment in Kaimuki became available after a renter moved out, I moved back in. I set up everything as it had been before, surrounding myself with mementos of our life together. I fully intended for this to be the last of the eighteen relocations in my adult life! Yet I felt restless and yearned to revisit cherished people and places. In early April I spent four months in Europe where I felt I was able to convey Genevieve's goodbyes to her loved ones on her behalf. I was engulfed in sadness without her, but I returned home satisfied that I had made my last trip abroad, knowing that at eighty-one years old, such travel was too tiring for me to manage again.

Once settled at home, I always found plenty to keep me occupied. I organized my scrapbooks and albums, read a lot, attended computer classes at the Apple Store, and substitute taught during the school year. I didn't feel ready to mix with new friends, so I limited my socializing to extended family. I enjoyed cooking my "famous" ratatouille dish and escargot dinners in my apartment, inviting Eric, Sharon, and Talisa to join me.

In time I was ready to get out a bit, to attend church functions and make new friends. The people I met were like me: active seniors who were widowed or otherwise single. I began to think how nice it would be to have someone compatible and age-appropriate with whom to go out for dinner or a movie.

I met a Canadian woman who offered to drive so we could go out for a nice meal. During our dinner conversation she expressed an interest in attaining U.S. citizenship. As she drove me home, she turned in front of another car and had a bad fender-bender. The other car was so badly damaged that it had to be towed away. We were unharmed, but it frightened me because I didn't see well enough to anticipate the collision. The accident didn't faze her much at all. I didn't schedule any more dates with her, as she wasn't my type.

Another lady, this one around my age and of Italian descent, was interesting and friendly. We met several times, but always in social groups with others. In a quiet moment, she casually told me, "I've had an elderly boyfriend for several years, but we don't have any exclusive arrangement. I can go out with other people if I wish." Her candid disclosure caught me by surprise. My mind began to conjure up images of getting caught in a geriatric love triangle and some jealous old geezer stalking me with a gun. I bailed out of this relationship like a passenger from a burning boat.

I accepted a dinner invitation to meet a "very special" widowed lady at the home of a friend of a friend. I wasn't given any other information. That is, I did not have a name or a description of the woman I was going to meet. When my friend was a no-show due to an unforeseen problem, I didn't know anyone else there, so I milled about aimlessly, nibbling on hors d'oeuvres, and introducing myself to strangers. I finally sat down despondently in a corner by myself. Feeling guilty about being a party pooper, I went outside to the lanai where several women were talking. As I headed in their direction, three of them quickly stood up, excused themselves, and went into another room. I didn't want to take their sudden exit personally but I wondered if I had spilled something on my shirt or, worse, my pants. I sat down bravely next to the only person still there, a strikingly pretty Asian lady with big, bright eyes. Her name was Alice, and we engaged in small talk for a while about food, the weather, and the standard "where you're from" conversation. I began to feel comfortable, more like myself. Curious about her connection to the party's hosts, I asked, "So, what is it that brings you here tonight?" She looked back at me with mild surprise and said, "I was invited here to meet you." With a relieved laugh, my embarrassment dissolved in a split second because Alice was so kind and sweet. She said I could call her, which I most certainly did.

Although I had thought I was comfortably settled in my apartment, a series of flooding incidences, just after getting settled, told me otherwise. On more than one occasion I walked into my ground floor apartment to find myself standing in smelly water an inch deep. The flood, caused by overhead pipes bursting, overflowing, or leaking, damaged the carpets, flooring, and furniture. Building management had undergone a high rate of staff turnover and was slow to assess the damage and fix the problem. The situation became so tiresome that I decided to move again.

Given my age, I thought it would be prudent to return to OKSL, even if I still had painful memories of Genevieve passing away there. It gave me good access to medical care and I knew many of the cheerful, upbeat people that resided in the twenty-story building, as well as the friendly staff. My rent included meals and basic housekeeping services. Another plus was the convenience of the area: a major grocery store was located across the street and restaurants were within walking distance.

I rented a fifth-floor apartment and once again set it up with all my furnishings, covering every inch of wall space with framed family photos, Genevieve's artwork, and other paintings of sentimental value. It looked like an eclectic gallery, but being surrounded with precious memories made it homey.

Alice and I had been seeing each other for several months, enjoying social dinners and family gatherings. Looking for opportunities to be useful, I offered to do handyman work around her house. I undertook projects, such as building a fence, installing wiring, fixing hinges, and trimming trees, while she cooked wonderful meals for us. She also did the driving, picking me up and taking me home, whenever we had plans together. She was so vibrant with such a healthy attitude that my sense of contentment returned, and I had a new lease on life.

Despite my move, I continued to have bad luck with my living situation, particularly as it related to water. Due to faulty plumbing at OKSL, the kitchen drains in the apartments stacked directly above mine backed up. The water overflowed from their apartments to mine, soaking the carpet and floor. Entering my apartment to find squishy water everywhere became a recurring nightmare. Again, management's response disappointed me, as I waited weeks for cleanup and repairs. As the end of my one-year lease approached, I began looking at other apartments around town, wanting to be more conveniently located to Alice.

Committed to relocate, I signed a lease on the only available apartment that had all the features I wanted. It also had nearly 1,700 square feet of living space. That's a lot for one person. Two OKSL apartments could easily have fit into my new place on a high floor of The Regency at Kahala. Even after I had moved in everything I owned, space begged to be filled and my footsteps echoed, as I went from room to room. The regal building stands alone in a neighborhood of single-family homes. It towers over its surroundings, appearing to be at the same level as nearby mountains. Stunning views from the spacious lanai were wasted on me because daylight blinded me, as a result of my advancing macular degeneration. I invited over friends and family to dine and enjoy the view, however.

For many years I had kept the same home phone number listed in the local directory. Occasionally, I received a call from someone who had looked me up, but this hadn't happened much recently. Then a surprise call came from a former fifth-grade student. "Mr. DeCarlo? From SHAPE Elementary School in Belgium?" he asked. "This is Tyler Smith. I was one of your students twenty-five years ago, and I'm here visiting Hawaii!" I remembered Tyler. How wonderful of him to call! We had dinner together and reminisced about his fifth grade class, discussing life and the passage of time. I had to ask: "Did you ever open the paper mache shark-puppet head with my note inside?" "I kept it," he assured me. "But it is still unopened." Frankly, I didn't recall what I wrote about Tyler, only that I had predicted success for all of my students. Tyler had recently completed his service in the Navy and had begun attending Harvard Business School. Seeing how happy he was with his life and his plans for the future, I believed that the extra time and effort I had dedicated to enriching the academic experience for my students had been worthwhile.

***

I began this book telling about my mother and dad and their six children. From these eight people have come a total of fifty-two family members to date. Talk about a population explosion! Overall, the longevity of our family is impressive as well. Mother passed away in 1995 when she was ninety-four-years old, in the Florida nursing home where she had been living for several years. At that time I was in Belgium trying to close out the school year before my retirement, and unfortunately I couldn't attend her service. Dad passed away at the age of seventy-six from complications after suffering a stroke. My parents were remarkable people who gave their children the best possible start in life. I always keep loving memories of them in my heart.

Being a member of an Italian family means having lots of relatives. As my family continues to grow, we maintain our close ties, even from a distance.

My oldest brother Tony and his wife Antoinette had their first daughter, Rosemarie, followed by fraternal twins Frankie and Judy. All three of Tony's children are now middle-aged with a total of eleven children and seventeen grandchildren. Tony developed and applied his abilities as a machinist to become very successful, and was always in great demand by his employers.

My sister Evelyn became an executive secretary with Bell Telephone in their stockholder's department, and stayed with her job until retirement. Evelyn's only child is a daughter, Donna Jean. Evelyn and Donna Jean are still living in New Jersey.

Victor became an engineer and worked at the atomic bomb plant in Oakridge, Tennessee. Victor met his wife "Jo" at Oakridge, and they remained married for life but didn't have children.

Neil started his career as an appliance repairman and worked his way up to become a top salesman for Westinghouse in Florida, winning awards for his record-breaking sales. He and his wife Joan are still living in Florida and have four grown daughters;

Carolyn, Susan, Nancy, and Cynthia. Neil and Joan now have six grandchildren and five great-grandchildren.

Jean worked as an executive secretary for a chemical plant in New Jersey, where she met her husband Denny, a chemical engineer. They had two sons: Daniel, my namesake, and David. Denny passed away, but Jean and her son David are both living in New Jersey. Daniel lives in Florida with his wife.

As of 2015 I've also lost two of my brothers. Tony passed away at ninety-two-years old, and Victor tragically drowned at the age of eighty-five while still in good health. He and Jo had retired in Hawaii thirty years earlier, well before we arrived. They joined me for dinner regularly in the OKSL dining room where we caught up on news of our relatives on the east coast. One day I couldn't reach them to confirm our dinner plans, and it seemed strange when Victor didn't return my call. When Jo called me back later that night, she had shocking news. She said they had gone to the beach at Ala Moana Park for Victor's regular swim. He went into the water while she relaxed with a book. When she looked up, a crowd had formed on the beach nearby. Walking over to see what was going on, she found Victor unconscious on the sand surrounded by lifeguards applying CPR, but they failed to resuscitate him. My heart fell right to the floor at Jo's words. My brother was gone, just like that. He was strong, slim, healthy, and a very skilled swimmer. For him to drown was simply unbelievable.

As the old saying goes, there are a few bad apples on every tree. But our family has been very fortunate. I've had the best family for which anyone could ever wish. Our wise, hard-working parents were God's gift to us, and I give them full credit for all that we have become and achieved.

***

I have met many remarkable people in my life, and greatly admire those who persevere despite being handicapped. The most extraordinary person I've ever met was a man by the name of Milton, who I met while riding the bus to do my substitute teaching jobs in Honolulu. We became acquainted and I learned that

Milton had been blind since birth. He used his white cane to efficiently tap his way along sidewalks, over curbs, and onto the city bus which transported him to his job at the Honolulu Center for the Blind. He could read Braille and enjoyed listening to audio books. Milton had a keen sense of hearing, and listened for oncoming cars before safely crossing streets. He went all around the area to grocery and drugstores to do his shopping. Milton traveled alone to the mainland to attend conventions for the blind. His courage was astounding, to be able to do all these things and not be able to see. I asked how he could do all this without being discouraged, and he said, "Well, I don't feel sorry for myself...I accept what life has given me, and I go on."

As I tell this story, I am slowly going blind due to macular degeneration, and apparently no cures may be found in my lifetime. I can no longer do the reading, writing, and research I always enjoyed. I can't see in bright sunlight, and consequently must wear dark glasses and a hat when I go outside into the beautiful Hawaiian sunshine. I walk to the grocery store after dark, when it's easier for me to see. I only hope that when the time comes that I can no longer see, I will remember Milton and how he inspired me with his courage.

I conclude this account of my life of eighty-five years so-far, with the abundant satisfaction of having finally told my life story. It's gratifying to see these events in writing, whether heartwarming or traumatic. Along the way, I was given multiple second chances in life for which I am truly thankful. I married my dear Genevieve, the love of my life and a wonderful mother to our son, Eric. I am grateful for the opportunities that were given to me, and I tried to make the best of them. I will always be grateful to the teachers, friends, family, and even strangers who supported and helped me. Without them, I wouldn't have accomplished much of any value. I hope that I've made a difference and will leave this world a better place.

EPILOGUE

Words of Wisdom

My experiences in Libya brought home to me human nature in its rawest form. In my efforts to save another man's life, I almost lost my own and created an international incident. My actions were judged as a criminal act, and misjudged as a selfish act, with accusations that I did it only for money. I didn't. Government authorities simply couldn't believe that an individual in this day and age would actually put his life on the line to help rescue another person.

I helped my friend because his life was in danger. He was a Jew, but I would have helped him whether he was an Arab, a rich man, a poor man, or black or white. The only thing that mattered to me was he was my friend. Six months after the Libya incident, we traveled from D.C. to New York to meet with Alphonso's brother at his request, as he was in the U.S. for a business trip. He thanked us profusely for having saved his brother's life. If I had to do it over again, would I? My answer is, "Yes."

In other areas of my career, I saw wanton fraud, abuse, and corruption by those entrusted with power and in positions of high authority. I have never, in all of my life, seen such bumbling in situations that could have been easily handled by someone with but a smidgeon of competence. Watch what they do, not what they say! Regrettably, I feel that some of the officials I dealt with in the State Department, the military, and the education department would have sold their own mother if needed to accomplish their political and personal agendas.

I paid a price, however, as the retributions for my actions were punitive in the extreme. I almost lost my life and my family. I sacrificed my position and career status, a considerable amount of hard-earned money, and my family was put through a great deal of pain, anguish, and suffering. The mental and physical stresses we endured took their toll and that was a real tragedy. Was it worth the price? My answer is, "Yes."

These negatives were more than balanced by the love of my family and the inspiration of young people, educators, friends, and caregivers everywhere. You are indeed God's angels on earth. Also, to so many who in one way or another guided, assisted, and encouraged me along the journey, I thank you deeply. I made it because of you. And finally to our great country, the United States of America, which provides opportunities to those who are willing to work and, in spite of some difficulties, succeed and prosper.

I conclude with a remembrance of Genevieve, whose beauty, charm, and wit captivated my heart. Also of my Mother, whose advice, "Oh, son, you'd better watch those French girls" provided the title of this book. Little did we realize the meaning of those words, and how her prediction would come true!

LESSONS FROM A LIFE WELL-LIVED

Looking more than eight decades in the rear-view, what life-lessons can I share? My overall message, primarily directed at young people who I think will most benefit, is that the present casts its shadow far into the future. If you are young, in time you will be old. Those who are old were once young. The choices you make, and ultimately the person you become, are your responsibility. In that regard, the wisdom I have to offer may be of permanent importance.

- *On wisdom.* Simply to know is not to be wise. To be wise is to apply common sense, prudence, and good judgment to things that matter. Recognizing when a decision is important and deserves your attention implies an understanding of situations, people, values, and one's self. Wisdom is an accumulated skill and is acquired slowly through experience. Learn to develop it.

- *On integrity.* Senator Alan Simpson said, "If you have integrity, nothing else matters. If you don't have integrity, nothing else matters." Associate with those of good quality because your reputation is your greatest asset. It takes years to cultivate but can be compromised in a minute. Reflect on your reputation and always strive to give your best.

- *On thinking.* Youth prefer to see the world as black and white and are tempted by the idea that everything that happens to them is controllable. They are often in error but never in doubt! Listen to your gut but don't let emotions overpower your logic. Thinking in shades of gray is a sign of maturity, but it is hard and requires discipline.

- *On education.* Although education doesn't determine intelligence or guarantee a job, the uneducated are always placed at a great disadvantage. No matter how much natural ability you may have, if you are ignorant, you are discounted. Education is your passport to opportunity. Experience is inevitable, learning is not.

- *On older people.* Most older people, and the older the better, know important things. They are experts in some things, deeply experienced in others, insightful in all. Older people offer kernels of wisdom, knowledge valued not because it comes from their authority, but because it comes from their own struggles to learn how the world turns. Listen to what they say. Learn from the bad; assimilate the good; discard the rest.

- *On success.* Live long and well by making healthy choices. Education, good habits, hard work and persistence, common sense, and taking responsibility are your best allies to achieving the American dream. Learn from the mistakes of others—you don't have the time, energy, and money to make them all yourself.

- *On family and friends.* Remember those who care about you. There are very few of them. No one makes it alone because somebody—a parent, a teacher, a friend, or even a stranger—placed a bet on you. Write down the people, places, and events that have changed the course of your life. The results may surprise you.

- *On happiness.* Devote time and energy to relationships. Express humility, show gratitude, and offer forgiveness. Be motivated about something and develop a sense of duty and accomplishment. Follow your heart, not the money. Think positively and exercise your body. Volunteer. Cultivate faith and take time to conscientiously count your blessings once a week. Don't look backwards for very long. Keep moving forward, open new doors, and find new inspirations. And what shall you make of this moment? Live, and love, like there's no tomorrow!

APPENDIX

The Joy of Growing Up Italian

Close Calls and Life-Changing Circumstances

The Boy Scouts of America: A Wonderful Organization

My Favorite Poems and Sayings

Talisa's Quotations and Eye Injury

Greetings from Harold Harlow Corbin

Escargots a la DeCarlo: The Recipe

The essay below has been around for many years, and there are several versions; none of them attributed to any named author. As a child of Italian immigrants, I had these same experiences and enjoy the humor of this writing, so I'm sharing it here.

The Joy of Growing up Italian

I was well into adulthood before I realized that I was an American. Of course, I had been born in America and had lived here all my life. But somehow it never occurred to me that just being a citizen of the United States meant I was an American. Americans were people who ate peanut butter and jelly on mushy white bread that came in plastic packages. Me? I was Italian. For me—as I am sure for most second generation Italian-American children who grew up in the 40's and 50's—there was a definite distinction drawn between Us and Them. We were Italians. Everybody else; the Irish, Polish, Germans, and Jewish, they were the "MED-E'GONES." There was no animosity involved in that distinction. No prejudices, no hard feelings, just well... we were sure ours was the better way.

For instance, we had a bread man, a coal and ice man, a fruit & vegetable man and a fish man; we even had a man who sharpened knives and scissors who came to our home or at least right outside our home. They were the many peddlers who plied the Italian neighborhoods. We would wait for their call, their yell, their individual distinctive sound. We knew them all and they knew us. Americans went to the stores for most of their foods—what a waste! Truly, I pitied their loss. They never knew the pleasure of waking up every morning to find a hot crisp loaf of Italian bread

203

waiting behind the screen door. And instead of being able to climb up on the back of a peddler's truck a couple of times a week just to hitch a ride, most of my "MED-E'GONE" friends had to be satisfied going to the A&P. When it came to food, it always amazed me that my American friends or classmates only ate turkey on Thanksgiving or Christmas. Or rather, that they only ate turkey, stuffing, mashed potatoes and cranberry sauce. We Italians, we also had turkey, stuffing, mashed potatoes and cranberry sauce. But only after we had finished the antipasto, soup, lasagna, meatballs, salad and whatever else Mama thought might be appropriate for that particular holiday. The turkey was usually accompanied by a roast of some kind (just in case somebody walked in who didn't like turkey) and was followed by an assortment of fruit, nuts, pastries, cakes, and of course, homemade cookies.

No holiday was complete without some home baking; none of that store bought stuff for us. This is where you learned to eat a seven-course meal between noon and 4 PM. We knew to handle hot chestnuts, and to put peach wedges in homemade red wine. I truly believe Italians live a romance with food.

Speaking of food, Sunday was truly the big day of the week. That was the day you'd wake up to the smell of garlic and onions frying in olive oil. As you lay in bed, you could hear the hiss of tomatoes dropping into a pan. On Sundays we always had gravy (what the MED E'GONES called sauce) and macaroni, which they called pasta.

Sunday would not be Sunday without going to mass. Of course, you couldn't eat before mass because you had to fast before receiving communion. But, the good part was we knew when we got home we'd find hot meatballs frying, and nothing tastes better than newly fried meatballs and crisp Italian bread dipped into a pot of gravy.

There was another difference between Us and Them. We had gardens...not just flower gardens, but huge gardens where we grew tomatoes, tomatoes, and more tomatoes. We ate them, cooked them, and jarred them. Of course, we also grew peppers, basil, lettuce and squash. Everybody had a grapevine and a fig tree and in the fall everyone made homemade wine, lots of it. Of course, those gardens thrived because we also had something else it seemed our American friends didn't seem to have. We had a grandfather!! It's not that they didn't have grandfathers, its just that they did not live in the same house or on the same block. They visited their grandfathers. We ate with ours and God forbid we didn't see him at least once a day. I can still remember my grandfather telling me how he came to America as a young man "on the boat," and how the family lived in a rented tenement and took in boarders in order to make ends meet. He decided he didn't want his children—five sons and two daughters—to grow up in that environment. All of this we learned, spoken in his own version of Italian-English which I soon learned to understand quite well.

So, when he saved enough, and I could never figure out how, he bought a house. That house served as family headquarters for the next forty years. I remember how he hated to leave the house and would rather sit on the back porch and watch the garden grow. When he did go out for some special occasion, he had to return as quickly as possible. After all, "nobody's watching the house."

I also remember the holidays when all the relatives would gather at my grandfather's house and there'd be tables full of food and homemade wine and music. Women in the kitchen, men in the living room and kids, kids everywhere. I must have a half million cousins; first, second and some that aren't even related, but what did it matter? And my grandfather, his pipe in his mouth and his fine mustache trimmed, would sit in the middle of it all grinning his mischievous smile, his dark eyes twinkling, surveying his domain, proud of his family and how well his children had done in life. One was a cop, one a fireman, one had his trade and of course there was always the rogue. The girls, they had all married well and had fine husbands and healthy children and everyone knew RESPECT.

He had achieved his goal in coming to America and to New York, and now his children and their children were achieving those same goals that were available to them in this great country because they were Americans.

When my grandfather died years ago at the age of 76, things began to change. Slowly at first, but then uncles and aunts eventually began to cut down on their visits. Family gatherings were fewer and something seemed to be missing, although when we did get together, usually at my mother's house now, I always had the feeling he was there somehow. It was understandable of course. Everyone now had families of their own and grandchildren of their own. Today they visit once or twice a year. Today we meet at weddings and wakes.

Lots of other things have changed too. The old house my grandfather bought is now covered with aluminum siding, although my uncle still lives there and of course my grandfather's garden is gone. The last of the homemade wine has long since been drunk and nobody covers the fig trees in the fall anymore. For a while we would make the rounds on the holidays, visiting family. Now, we occasionally visit the cemetery. A lot of them are there; grandparents, uncles, aunts, even my own father and mother.

The holidays have changed too. The great quantity of food we once consumed without ill effects is no good for us anymore. To much starch, too much cholesterol, too many calories, and nobody bothers to bake anymore. Too busy. It's easier to buy it now, and too much is no good for you. We meet at my house now, or at least my family does, but it's not the same.

The difference between Us and Them isn't so easily defined anymore, and I guess that's good. My grandparents were Italian-Italians, my parents were Italian-Americans, I'm an American-Italian, and my children are American-Americans. Oh, I'm an American all right and proud of it, just as my grandfather would want me to be. We are all Americans now—the Irish, Germans, Poles, and Jews. U.S. citizens all, but somehow I still feel a little bit Italian. Call it culture, call it tradition, call it roots, I'm really not sure what it is. All I do know is that my children have been cheated out of a wonderful piece of heritage. They never knew my grandfather.

~ *anonymous*

Close Calls and
Life-Changing Circumstances

When I was around eight years old, my mother was carrying a pot of boiling hot water from the stove to a wash tub. I was running from my brother and came down the stairs to the cellar. I didn't look at what my mom was doing, I just dashed under her arms. Bumping into Mother caused the hot water to spill onto my neck and shoulder, and I began screaming in pain. Luckily Dad was home, and he immediately ran to the back yard to mix a mud paste and apply it to the blistering burns. It worked! I was relieved of pain and there were no aftereffects.

One day when I was about ten, I fell and got a deep cut on my left knee. I wasn't far from home so I got there as fast as I could. Dad looked at my wound and went quickly to the cellar, returning with a big spider web hanging from a stick. There were always spider webs in the dark corners of our cellar. He quickly applied the web to the rather large cut, and the bleeding stopped. Many years later I told a doctor about this and he explained that spider webs contain a coagulant which sealed the cut and stopped the bleeding. And there was no infection or blood poisoning, when you think about the dust and dirt on that spider web! I still have the scar on my left knee.

Another scary circumstance was when my kid brother Neil followed me to my friend's house. I was around ten years old, and Neil was about six. My friend lived about two blocks from our home, on the other side of Chestnut Avenue, a main road. I didn't know he was following me but as I entered my friend's house, on the other side of the street we heard the screeching of tires. We ran outside and saw Neil laying on the road, hit by a car! My friend's dad picked up Neil, who was not moving, and drove him to the hospital. Neil sustained only a broken leg. I thought we would lose him because of me.

Another incident involved my brother Victor, when I was around eleven years old. We were in the back yard, arguing about what movie we should go see, when we started fighting and pushing each other. Our large glass cellar window was on the ground floor and as we fought, we didn't notice how close we had come to it until we both went crashing through the window, shattering the glass. We were covered with glass shards, as was the floor. Mother came running with a broom, used both for cleaning up the glass and for whacking us, which we deserved.

During my college years, in the summers and Christmas holidays I worked in the mail sorting warehouse for Lackawanna Railroad. There was a huge sorting room where packages would come down a chute. We'd pick them up, look at the address and then walk them over to another chute to be delivered to a box-car going to that state. One night during on the graveyard shift I was working in the open warehouse at the waterfront, and it was so cold I wore several jackets, pairs of pants, gloves, hats and scarves... it was freezing! I picked up a box addressed to Ohio, hoisted it onto my shoulder and walked over to toss it down the chute. In a few minutes, I smelled something burning! The smell came from my jacket and gloves, which were smoking and disintegrating on my body! In a panic I tore off my gloves and jacket and the extra pair of pants. The other men came over to see what was going on and we realized that the package contained a leaking battery and the acid had spilled down my clothing. It was illegal to ship car batteries for that reason, but someone did it anyway! I was so lucky that the caustic acid hadn't spilled on my face, eyes, or bare skin, as I may have been blinded or scarred for life. It was a close call I would not wish on anyone, and I'm so grateful I was spared!

During high school I was on the wrestling team, and in those days the mats were made of canvas and they got really sweaty and grimy. After a practice match, I received a couple of mat burns on each elbow. I thought nothing of it, so I washed my arms and let the scabs form. After a few days, each of my arms had formed a red line, going up to my armpits. They hurt, but I believed I was tough, and let it go. The next night I showed the red lines to my mother as I was going to bed. I was tired and just wanted to get some sleep, but she said, "No way. Get dressed right now, we're going to the hospital."

She insisted, so I got dressed reluctantly and we walked up to the hospital at about eleven o'clock. The emergency room doctor asked me to hold up my arms, and he pulled a large scab off each arm. I let out a huge yell and my eyes teared. He put some medication on the wounds, bandaged me up and told me to sit down and wait. I then heard him say in a very serious tone to my mother, "It's a good thing you brought him in tonight, Ma'am, as he would have been dead in the morning." This frightened me to no end when I heard this. The red lines were blood poisoning, and in another six hours I would have been gone. Mother knows best.

At Newark Boy's Vocational and Technical High School, I ran for student body president. The English teacher who sponsored the student council didn't like me. I gave a campaign promise to oust the current council sponsor if I won, so she closed the elections early when she found out I was winning! This gave her time to solicit more votes for the other candidate, who she preferred. I protested to the vice principal, Mr. Wagner, who then re-ran the election, which I won with a large majority. Some of my buddies had a singing quartet and we did a jingle for my campaign: "We want DeCarlo, we want him bad. Vote for DeCarlo and you won't be sad. When you vote, make sure you vote for DeCarlo, he's the man we want, rah-rah-rah!" The jingle was silly, but the opportunity to be student body president was a wonderful experience for me.

The amazing double-coincidence of having both our friends no-show for lunch on my first day in Paris made it possible for me to meet Genevieve. I am humbly grateful for this occurrence. I didn't know it at the time, but I had just met the joy of my life.

I married the first French woman I met, and it was the best thing I ever did.

Soon after arriving in Italy, Genevieve and I took a trip by car and were driving to Rome on an early February morning. Not far from Verona, we hit a patch of black ice. I'd heard of it, but had no experience with this dangerous hazard. When we hit the ice, I lost control of the car and we spun around and around. Luckily for us, no other cars were on the road at the time, or it would have been a terrible pile-up. As we spun around for three or four times, I got control of the car and was able to stop, but not before the living daylight was frightened out of us. That was my first and last experience with black ice. It could have been the last of us!

Another brush with danger was on a trip to Denmark on the German autobahn. I was driving our rear-engine Renault Dauphine when I smelled gasoline. I stopped to check the motor but didn't see anything unusual. We drove on, but the odor continued and disturbed us, so again I stopped, and this time spotted a leak under the gas tank. Luckily the gas leak didn't reach the hot motor, but there were no repair stations in sight. I then remembered what a friend once told me about gas leaks: "Take a bar of soap and rub it over the leak. It should stop it." I did just that, with a bar of soap from our luggage. It worked! I drove over three thousand kilometers with a soap-patch sealing the gas tank leak. I had it repaired as soon as I could.

On a trip through Yugoslavia in the early 1960s, we were driving through a scenic mountain area and stopped to eat a lunch we brought along. We returned to the car and when I put the key in the lock to open it, the key broke off! We had a second key, but it was in our luggage in the locked car. I didn't want to break the window or door, but fortunately there was a "wind-wing" side window, and I easily broke the latch, reached into the car and opened the door. But unfortunately we found this to be a fault of the car's design. I had the window latch fixed, but not long after, we made a lunch stop in Paris on the Champs-Elysees with all our luggage and cameras locked in the car. We stepped away for no more than twenty minutes, and came back to find that little side window open and all our belongings gone! We went to the police and filled out the papers, but they gave us little hope, as they had hundreds of these reports every day in Paris. I had many wonderful photos of our European trip in those cameras, never to be seen again.

On our way via train from Verona to Genoa, I was busy getting our bags off the train when six-year old Eric jumped off to wait for us on the platform. As Genevieve and I were about to step off, the doors suddenly closed and the train began to move out of the station! We were horrified as we saw Eric looking back at us, standing alone on the platform and holding his stuffed toy tiger. I was about to pull the emergency cord when the conductor told me, "Don't do that! There's a big fine for stopping the train! Just get off at the next stop and come back." I yelled through the window to Eric, "Wait here for us, we'll come back!" Helplessly, we remained on the train until the next stop and grabbed a taxi to hurry back, but he was already gone! We asked where to find the carabinieri (police) and were directed to an office nearby. We walked in to find unflappable Eric, sitting atop a police desk and chatting in Italian with five laughing carabinieris who were greatly entertained by the Italian-speaking Eric. They told us he was an adorable bambino! What a relief to find him. I dreaded to think what could have happened.

While driving along the highway to Rome, we got stuck following a large livestock hauler full of cattle. I had the Renault's sliding roof open and decided to pass the truck the first chance we had. Just before pulling around the truck to pass, I closed the roof because it was too windy. Just then, a wall of smelly fresh cow dung and urine hit our windshield with a giant smack! My sight was momentarily obscured, but I used the wipers and could barely see through the brown-smeared windshield to continue driving. We pulled over at the next station and had to wash the car before continuing on, and found that the manure was also covering the sunroof which I had closed moments before impact, inadvertently saving our vacation from ruin.

In Libya, we enjoyed traveling around the country to visit the sights. The dancing men of the Tuareg tribe performed for their occasional visitors in darkness around a campfire, and we felt very fortunate to observe this ancient tradition. As we sat watching the dancers, through the flickering firelight I spotted a tribal member on the opposite side of the campfire who suddenly picked up a stone and came running towards me! He was so fast, there was no time for me to react or get out of his way. Holding the stone tightly, he flicked it across the leg of my pants, crying out in alarm as he pointed to a black scorpion crawling away on the ground. Black scorpions are legendary in Libya, and their stings are deadly. The man's quick action may have saved me from a painful death.

While we were living in Laon France, Genevieve had washed the dishes and placed them in the dish rack without realizing a knife was upright with the blade sticking up. As she was working around the sink area, she bent over the the dish drainer and the knife blade grazed her head along her temple, an inch from her eye. When I arrived home she was visibly shaken at how close she came to injuring herself. She never made that mistake again!

While moving into our house on Okinawa, I unpacked a lamp and plugged it in but it didn't work. I walked over to flip on the wall switch and the outlet gave a little explosion, because it was a 280v high-voltage plug, and it burned the plug and wire all the way up to the lamp! If the wall switch had been on when I turned on the lamp while holding it, I would have been fried!

A "ten-second life saver" occurred while we were living on Okinawa and Genevieve booked a flight to France to attend her mother's funeral. While changing planes at the airport in Beirut, passengers had to walk to another part of the airport by passing under tall scaffolding in front of a building. Genevieve's group had just cleared the scaffolding when it suddenly collapsed in a loud crash of wood, metal, and dust. If it had fallen ten seconds before, Genevieve and the others would have been severely injured or killed. Her life was saved by a few precious seconds.

During my assignment on Okinawa Island, I was in the staff lounge at Kubasaki High School where someone had left a large glass bottle of ginger ale on the countertop. I went into the room and took something out of the fridge, saw the bottle but didn't think anything of it, then walked back in and out again, passing that bottle twice within a few minutes. As I left the room to return to my office about eight feet away, there was an explosion in the lounge. Shattered glass came flying out of the lounge door with such force, glass shards were imbedded in the door and across the hallway in the walls! We had to dig out the glass from the door and walls with a screwdriver. My safety, and perhaps my life, were spared by a few seconds. I shudder to think what would have happened if I had been standing by that soda bottle when it blew up.

The Boy Scouts of America: A Wonderful Organization

By the age of ten I had worked my way up to "Second Class" rank in the Boy Scouts, and was about to take the test for First Class when we moved to Newark in 1944. I didn't continue with the scouts when we were in New Jersey, but I started up boy scout and sea scout troops while I was director of a youth center during my college years in Newberry, South Carolina. I've always believed in their mission and recommended that parents enroll their sons in programs offered by this organization.

At about the same time I was selected to teach in France, I was offered a position as state commissioner for the Boy Scouts chapter in South Carolina, but chose to move to France and thereafter remained in Europe for many years.

When I taught fourth grade from 1959-61 at Verona Elementary School in Italy, I formed a Boy Scout troop and we enjoyed hikes in the mountains. Our troop also participated in Verona's annual Mardi Gras Parade, pulling along our class art project, a tall paper mache giraffe on wheels. I bought thousands of pieces of gum in colorful wrappers, and the boys tossed the candy to delighted spectators. Many of the kids wore costumes, and I joined in the fun wearing giant glasses with a big plastic nose and mustache.

The parade crowds lined the same streets where ancient Romans and gladiators had marched to the nearby arena, and this setting added to the experience and made it all the more unforgettable.

Founded in 1910, The Boy Scouts of America (BSA) currently includes over three million active members. I admire The Scouts' values of teaching responsible citizenship, self-reliance, and

Verona's Mardi Gras parade and our class, including the Boy Scout troop

trustworthiness, which promote character development. The BSA's programs offer a wide variety of outdoor and community activities to help bring structure and direction to the lives of boys and young men. These qualities may inspire them to continue on into adulthood as valuable contributors to society.

My Favorite Sayings

Be ashamed to die until you have won some victory for humanity.
   ~ Horace Mann.

You can do anything you ought to do.
   ~ Dr. Bob Jones, Sr.

*It is no disgrace to fail; it is a disgrace to do less than your best to
   keep from failing.*
~ Dr. Bob Jones, Sr.

*Our task is to provide an education for the kind of kids we have... Not
   the kind of kids we used to have... Or want to have... Or the kids
   that exist in our dreams.*
   ~ Mary Kay Utech

The door to success swings on the hinges of good works.
   ~ Dan De Carlo

*Three keys to long life: A. Eat proper foods. B. Exercise. C. De-
   velop a sense of humor.*
   ~ Dan De Carlo

Only a Teacher

I am a teacher!
What I do and say are being absorbed by young minds
who echo those images across the ages.
My lessons will be immortal,
affecting people yet unborn,

people I will never see or know.
The future of the world is in my classroom today-
a future with the potential for good or bad.
The pliable minds of tomorrow's leaders will be molded
either artistically or grotesquely by what I do.

Several future presidents are learning from me today-
so are the great writers of the next decades
and so are the so-called ordinary people
who make the decisions in a democracy.
I must never forget these same people
could be the thieves and murderers of the future.

Only a teacher.
Thank God I have a calling to the greatest
profession of all.
I must be vigilant every day
lest I lose one fragile opportunity
to improve tomorrow.

— Dr. Ivan Fitzwater

Groovy, Man, Groovy

Remember when hippy meant big in the hips,
And a trip involved travel in cars, planes and ships?
When pot was a vessel for cooking things in
And hooked was what grandmother's rug might have been?
When fix was a verb that meant mend or repair,
And be-in meant merely existing somewhere?
When neat meant well organized, tidy and clean,
And grass was a ground cover, normally green?
When lights and not people were switched on and off,
And the pill might have been what you took for a cough?

When camp meant to quarter outdoors in a tent,
And pop was what the weasel went?

When groovy meant furrowed with channels and hollows
And birds were wing'd creatures, like robins and swallows?
When fuzz was a substance, real fluffy, like lint,
And bread came from bakeries—-not from the mint?
When square meant a 90-degree angled form,
And cool was a temperature not quite warm?
When roll meant a bun, and rock was a stone,
And hang-up was something you did with a phone?
When chicken meant poultry and bag meant a sack.
With junk trashy cast-offs and old bric-a-brac?
When jam was preserves that you spread on your bread,
And crazy meant balmy, not right in the head?

When cat was a feline, a kitten grown up,
And tea was a liquid you drank from a cup?
When swinger was someone who swung in a swing,
And pad was a soft sort of cushiony thing?
When way out meant distant and far, far away,
And a man couldn't sue you for calling him gay?
When tough described meat too unyielding to chew,
And making a scene was a rude thing to do?
Words once so sensible, sober and serious
Are making the freak scene, like psychodelirious.
It's groovy, man, groovy, but English it's not,
Methinks that our language is going to pot.

— Anonymous

When You Are Old

When you are old and grey and full of sleep,
And nodding by the fire, take down this book,
And slowly read, and dream of the soft look
Your eyes had once, and of their shadows deep;
How many loved your moments of glad grace,
And loved your beauty with love false or true,
But one man loved the pilgrim soul in you,
And loved the sorrows of your changing face;

And bending down beside the glowing bars,
Murmur, a little sadly, how Love fled
And paced upon the mountains overhead
And hid his face amid a crowd of stars.

— William Butler Yeats

Casey at the Bat

I memorized *Casey at the Bat* for a speech contest in college, giving a dramatized presentation to two thousand people and winning Honorable Mention. Wearing a baseball costume for effect, I enjoyed performing it countless times throughout my life; in school assemblies, variety shows, social gatherings, parties, USO shows, service clubs and officers clubs. I've included it for sentimental reasons, along with my dramatized preface and this classic baseball song to join in with before I did the reading:

Take me out to the ballgame,
Take me out with the crowd,
Buy me some peanuts and Cracker Jack,
I don't care if I never get back,
Let me root, root, root for the home team,
If they don't win it's a shame—

For it's one—two—three strikes you're out,
At the old ball game.

The story of Casey, by Earnest Thayer, was first published on June 3, 1888. Of all the fictional characters to come out of baseball, the one who held a place in the minds and hearts of fans was the great Casey-the-Slugger. No one yet has been able to say where he was born, where he lived, what position he played, if he hit left-handed or right, if he was a pull hitter, or what he could do with a spit ball. One thing does remain indelibly stamped in the minds of the baseball-loving public—Casey fanned the breeze with the bases loaded and lost Midville its pennant. Casey niched a place for himself in the imaginary hall of fame; not because of what he did, but rather because of what he failed to do.

There have been those who have wanted to hang him in effigy, and others who insisted he should have been tar-and-feathered, and burning at the stake was a popular demand. Some, with charity in their hearts, have asked for him to have a second chance, while others, in their imaginations, have brought back to life the happy Irishman, who in his incarnation, faced the same pitcher and lammed out a round-tripper to give Mudville a sure-enough pennant.

To many he was a hero, and to others he was a bum...and now: *Casey at the Bat*. Let's give a cheer for Casey!

Casey at the Bat

It looked extremely rocky for the Mudville nine that day
The score stood two to four, with but an inning left to play
So when Cooney died at second, and Burrows did the same
A pallor wreathed the features of the patrons of the game.

A struggling few got up to go, leaving there the rest
With that hope which springs eternal within the human breast.

For they thought, If only Casey could get a whack at that
They'd put up even money with Casey at the bat.

But Flynn preceded Casey, and likewise so did Blake
And the former was a puddin', and the latter was a fake
So on that stricken multitude a death-like silence sat
For there seemed but little chance of Casey getting to the bat.
But Flynn let drive a single to the wonderment of all
And the much despised Blakey tore the cover off the ball
And when the dust has settled and they saw what had occurred
There was Blakey safe at second, and Flynn a-huggin' third.

Then from the gladdened multitude went up a joyous yell —
It rumbled in the mountaintops, it rattled in the dell
It struck upon the hillside and rebounded on the flat
For Casey, Mighty Casey, was advancing to the bat.

There was ease in Casey's manner as he stepped into his place
There was pride in Casey's bearing and a smile on his face
And when responding to the cheers he lightly doffed his hat
No stranger in the crowd could doubt 'twas Casey at the bat.

Ten thousand eyes were on him as he rubbed his hands with dirt
Five thousand tongues applauded when he wiped them on his
* shirt*
When the writhing pitcher ground the ball into his hip
Defiance glanced in Casey's eyes, a sneer curled Casey's lips.

And now the leather-covered sphere came hurtling through the air
And stood a-watching it in haughty grandeur there
Close by the sturdy batsman the ball unheeded sped
That ain't my style, said Casey. Strike one, the umpire said.

From the benches, black with people, there went up a muffled roar
Like the beating of the storm waves on the stern and distant shore

Kill him! Kill the umpire! Shouted someone in the stand
And it's likely they'd have done it had not Casey raised his hand.

Like a smile of Christian charity great Casey's visage shone
He stilled the rising tumult, he made the game go on
He signaled to the pitcher and once more the spheroid flew
But Casey still ignored it, and the umpire said, Strike two.

Fraud! cried the maddened thousands, and the echo answered Fraud!
But one scornful look from Casey and the audience was awed
They saw his face grow stern and cold, they saw his muscles strain
And they knew that Casey wouldn't let the ball go by again.

The sneer is gone from Casey's lips, his teeth are clenched in hate
He pounds with cruel vengeance his bat upon the plate
And now the pitcher holds the ball, and now he lets it go
And now the air is shattered by the force of Casey's blow.

Oh, somewhere in this favored land, the sun is shining bright
The band is planing somewhere, and somewhere hearts are light
And somewhere men are laughing and somewhere children shout
But there is no joy in Mudville: Mighty Casey has struck out.

Talisa's Funny Quotations

When Talisa was about nine, we took her the dentist for some necessary teeth extractions and we could hear her crying out loudly in pain as we winced and worried from the waiting room. When she came out, she was holding her jaw and said in front of the dentist, his wife (the receptionist) and everyone; "Next time, I'm going to a professional!"

On a visit to Paris when Talisa was around four, we were in a hotel elevator on the 8th floor, coming down. The doors opened and lots of people got on, including one man with a large suitcase. We all had to move closer together to make room. Talisa whispered, "Why did he have to get on? There's no room in here." The man glanced down at her and replied, "Sorry about that." Talisa was quiet for a minute and then added, "It's a good thing there's a small person in here, or we'd all be squished!" Everyone laughed.

When Talisa was four and staying with us in Belgium, there were very steep steps leading up to her bedroom. As she climbed up the steps she called out, "These steps sure are steep! You could fall backwards while going up!"

And fortunately my feelings remained intact at this one: "You're too fat, Grandpa...I can't hug you."

She was watering the flowers while wearing new shoes. They got wet, and I said "Grandma is going to be mad." Talisa said, "We can tell her it was an accident...that we walked into the water. Oh no, we have to tell the truth, or we can pretend...oh no, we have to tell the truth. Will Grandma be mad at you, or me?"

"She'll be mad at me," I replied. Talisa said, "Ok, then we can tell her."

We all went out for ice cream and three cups were brought to the table; a large, a medium, and a small size. Talisa said, "The biggest one is for me!" and had it in her hands before we could even say a word.

I asked Talisa, "Did I tell you that I love you?" She said, "No, you didn't." "I love you," I said. "I love you, too," said Talisa. Later I heard her tell Genevieve, "I pretended he didn't tell me, but he did."

While visiting us at Le Quanty, we asked if Talisa might want us to invite over the neighbor's boys to play, but then added that they might play a little rougher than she did. She answered smartly, "Well, I'm a little bit rough too."

We were serving dessert and I asked her how much she wanted. She said, "I'll eat as much as I want…if I like it."

Talisa dropped her cup of milk and Grandma had to clean it up. I said, "Be careful." Genevieve then dropped a fork on the floor as we were eating. Talisa said, "I spill my milk, but Grandma drops a fork, and you didn't tell her to be careful."

Talisa asked about French terminology for women who are married or single; with madam as a "Mrs." and mademoiselle as a "Miss." "I'm young and not married, so that means I must be a 'missmoiselle,'" she observed.

We visited friends whose little daughter had a tantrum and received a sound scolding. On the way home, Talisa said, "Aren't you lucky you have a granddaughter like me?"

Talisa, when asked who Sharon was, answered "That's my mom, but she won't let me call her Sharon. That's why I hang out with my daddy."

Talisa was visiting us in France and asked if we had any stickers for her to play with. "We used them all up in Belgium." Talisa replied, "Didn't you think of Talisa when you moved to France?"

In the work shed: "You sure do have a lot of junk in here, Grandpa."

Talisa commenting on the rigors of obedience: "Sometimes I have to tell myself to say yes."

Talisa: "Why isn't the house clean?"
Dan: "I didn't have time."
Talisa: "Didn't you know I was coming?"

Talisa at age 4: "You should thank me for asking you to buy the duck, because ducks do a lot of doo-doo and your grass will grow."

During a tour of a medieval castle Talisa asked, "Why is the queen's bed larger than the king's bed? Is it because the queen is larger?"

While attending a ballet, we asked Talisa if she'd like to be a ballerina. She declared, "Oh no, I want to be a hula dancer!"

We were getting ready to go visit some friends and we told Talisa a boy her age would be there. She asked what to wear and Genevieve, thinking they'd want to be outside playing, said, "You can wear your jeans." Talisa countered, saying she wanted to wear a dress; "Don't you want me to look pretty?"

***

Reflections of my White Scar
by Talisa DeCarlo

In the 9th grade, supporting a member of my soccer family in the crowd of "Hawaii Stars," the bright lights started to bother my eye. My left eye felt dry and irritated as if an eyelash was under my contact lens. For the rest of the night I couldn't get rid of the pain. I wanted to see my optometrist, Dr. Shibata, but my mom thought I should wait until morning. The pain was so severe, it hurt whether I had my eye opened or closed. It was almost impossible to sleep.

In the morning I called Dr. Shibata immediately. When I came in, I learned I had an ulcer very close to the pupil of my eye. Bacteria were eating away my eye and had I not come in to the doctor's office within a couple of hours, I would have gone blind. Dr. Shibata gave me drops of antibiotics and steroids to put in my eye each hour. I wanted to overdose because the pain was excruciating. The drops helped to kill some of the bacteria and numb the pain. However, when I came in the next day, I was informed that the problem was beyond Dr. Shibata's expertise and I would have to see an ophthalmologist, Dr. Jenkins. She examined both of my eyes to make sure my right eye hadn't been infected as well. She gave me more drops and explained to me their purpose. She terrified me by telling me that if I forgot to put in the drops, I would go blind owing to the bacteria's proximity to the pupil of my eye. At that moment, I realized I really am not invincible. The consequences were very real to me.

That week was the longest of my life. I had to put in drops every half-hour during the day and every hour at night. My mom woke up throughout each night, prying open my eye. During the day, she stayed home to make sure I remembered to put in my drops. Although, I don't see how I could have forgotten. All I could do each day was lie around, counting down the time until the next pain-relieving drop. The world looked opaque white and my eyes were constantly dilated from the reflection off the white scar forming on my eye. Only as the pain lessened and my vision slowly improved could I start to do my unfinished homework. When I finally went in for my last check-up with Dr. Jenkins, I was convinced I wanted to become an ophthalmologist. I was, and still am, so grateful for what she did for me. I may have been just one of her many patients, but her actions had an immeasurable impact on my life. Some people may consider my suffering horrifying, yet I embrace it as the blessing in disguise as it has proven to be. This eye-opening experience has made me want to give back and help others who have vision-threatening ailments like mine. I aspire most fervently to one day wake up in the middle of the night to doctor someone with an ulcer or other eye emergency. If I could do that, at least once in my lifetime, I think my life would feel fulfilled.

Now, two and a half years later, all I have left is this fading scar. The small, white scar on my eye is a constant reminder of the scar on my heart, motivating me to always work hard and never take anything for granted.

Greetings from Harold Harlow Corbin

Mr. Harold Corbin, a famous lawyer from New York and a mutual friend, sent these New Year's greetings to us. Mr. Corbin defended the government officials involved in the famous "Teapot Dome" political bribery scandal of 1922. I thought they were very thought-provoking and therefore included them in this book.

Greetings from: HAROLD HARLOW CORBIN

12/16/1959

Congratulations and all happiness and good fortune to the De Carlos from Saturday forward forever—Harold

1958–1959

Friends: As this resolution for the coming year, I am submitting to you a Headmaster's Charge to his departing seniors last June. That his name is also mine may cast the shadow of pride—but not enough. I hope to relay some healthy and helpful sentiments which you may, or may not, fully share.

Charge of Headmaster Harold H. Corbin, Jr. to the 101st Class of Lake Forest Academy at the June 14, 1958 commencement:

"...And now, before you go, let me reiterate a caution or two.

"Beware the suspicion of quality in all your judgments, in all your thoughts, in all your actions. You will find the

world is full of this. Shun it as you would its handmaiden, provincialism of the mind and of the spirit.

"Learn to identify, seek to correct, but never descend to the insidious anti-intellectualism which has corrupted our educational system, vitiated our faith, and thus helped to tarnish the ideal of our democracy in the eyes of the world.

"Remember the sobering truth that 'civilization is the race between education and catastrophe.' In this race there are no ties; you either win or lose.

"Strive always for a just agreement in all your doings one with another, never forsake the good in your fellow men, but never, never be afraid to walk alone if walk alone you must.

"Remember, too, that if today you are great frogs in a very small pond, tomorrow you will be something less than tadpoles in a sea the size of which you cannot yet comprehend. To know this in advance won't change the situation, but it will help.

"Last, remember that in true humility lies your greatest strength, and that in the habitual contemplation of greatness you will soon find yourself, and, ultimately, God.

"And now I have done. God bless you. Come back as often as you can. I don't want you to go, believe me. As you do, you should know my conviction that you have helped lift our common enterprise, Lake Forest Academy, to new and unique levels of service. For this I am grateful above the strength of words to say."

1962–1963

Friends: We may find it hard to accept what lies beyond our understanding. But when going through some of life's dark tunnels, we should remember that they have light at both ends.

1963–1964

Friends: To speak, however loudly, against injustice, oppression and bigotry, is merely to state an ideal. To do justice, to deal fairly, to do away with prejudice is to live an ideal. It may be difficult to achieve; but we can try.

1964–1965

Friends: Discontentment is rife in this upside-down world; it may sober but must not rule our personal lives. For ourselves we can, at least, achieve the most and best in life by making the most and best of what we have. And this is contentment.

1965–1966

Friends: "Let us endure unflinchingly whatever sacrifices we are called upon to make to defend our free institutions from the right of communism, which is bent on undermining our faith in ourselves. Rely not only on the gold in our vaults, but the iron in our blood. And let us cling like ivy to the faith of our fathers until, in God's good time, all men are free." (from a recently published ad)

1965–1966

Friends: Genuine hospitality, a precious element of the holiday spirit, vibrates as a throb in the heart which cannot be described, but is immediately felt and puts the stranger at once at ease. It is a language the dumb can speak and the deaf can hear and understand. Let's indulge it to the full this year. —Helen and Harold Corbin, Round Lake, New York

1966–1967

Friends: For me to comment on the state of our world would merely tend uselessly to emphasize the horror and uncertainties of the times—hence a lighter reference to a book just published that assumes to describe a new standard of etiquette adopted by our "international nomad jet-set society":

"—Kissing is gaining momentum all the time xx Nomads adjudge it a direct, visual assertion of their social status xx It must be brief, on both cheeks, looking straight ahead xx and has no sexual connotation whatsoever xx Love life demands leisure, and this new breed of people has none."

1967–1968

Friends: It is a long accepted verity that we can do little with faith, but we can do nothing without it. Lack of faith connotes atheism—which resides rather in the lip than in the heart of man. Imagine the confusion of the atheist who, having cause to be grateful, looks about for someone to thank and finds that no one is there.

1968–1969

Friends: At this year's end I would supplement my seasonal greeting with a single thought—that the man never grows old who keeps a child in his heart.

1969–1970

Friends: Timothy Sexter, an American merchant (1747-1806), once wrote: "An ungrateful man is like a hog under a tree eating acorns, but never looking up to see where they come from."

ESCARGOTS A LA DECARLO

Have ready:

Ceramic baking dish with individual receptacles for escargots
2 dozen escargots from cans
1/4 lb. butter softened to room temperature
one handful fresh parsley leaves
3–8 cloves garlic, as you prefer
salt and pepper to taste

Directions:

1. Drain escargots in a strainer and rinse well.

2. Finely chop the parsley leaves and garlic, then mix with the butter to make a paste. Add salt and pepper to taste.

3. Place an escargot in each of the baking dish's receptacles and cover with the paste.

4. Place in oven at 350-400F for about 6 to 9 minutes or until sauce melts and sizzles.

5. Serve hot with French bread and red wine. Dip bread into the melted butter sauce.

Happy Snailing!

Comments, suggestions, and old friends are welcome!

For more photos, etc., search for *Daniel A. DeCarlo* on Face-book, or use this link: *https://www.facebook.com/profile.php?id=100005499525439&fref=ts*

You can also reach me at *mrdan1930@gmail.com.*

Dan